Performing Processes

Editor
Roberta Mock

intellect™
Bristol, UK
Portland OR, USA

First Published in Paperback in UK in 2000 by
Intellect Books, PO Box 862, Bristol BS99 1DE, UK

First Published in USA in 2000 by
Intellect Books, ISBS, 5824 N.E. Hassalo St, Portland, Oregon 97213-3644, USA

Consulting Editor: Masoud Yazdani
Cover Photograph: Sarah Swainson
Copy Editor: Jeremy Lockyer

A catalogue record for this book is available from the British Library

ISBN 1-84150-010-0

Cover Photograph (© Sarah Swainson):
Mark Shorto in Lusty Juventus's production of Shading the Crime (1998) by Christine Roberts.

Printed and bound in Great Britain by Cromwell Press, Wiltshire

Contents

The book is dedicated to our students

Introduction

Roberta Mock

'Finished, it's finished, nearly finished, it must be nearly finished.' *(Pause.)*

That Samuel Beckett knew a thing or two about the ontology of live performance is evident from the opening line of *Endgame*. The processes of writing are complete, the 'blueprint' finished. Following a pause for the full impact to sink in (moments of reception and reflection), the processes of presentation continue. I believe that Frost and Yarrow's observations on the work of Dario Fo can be applied to all live performance: "the play continues to be created every time it is performed" and, as such, the processes of presentation become fundamental "principles of construction".[1] A live performance, by its very nature, is always in the process of finishing: "While Waiting for Godot" (*En Attendant Godot*) is simultaneously by the author's own translation *Waiting for Godot*, both a process and a product. However, as Beckett's handling of thematic content exemplifies, it is usually more effective to 'show' rather than 'tell' when dealing with theoretical concepts.

Richard Schechner admits that "it is hard to define performance"[2]; my problems with his attempts in *Performance Theory* stem not simply from the fact that, as he notes, performance is the "broadest" and "most ill-defined disc" in his model of concentric overlapping circles and that he often uses the term itself as part of its own definition:

> the whole constellation of events, most of them passing unnoticed, that take place in/among both performers and audience from the time the first spectator enters the field of the performance – the precinct where the theater takes place – to the time the last spectator leaves.[3]

Such ambiguity and imprecision make it impossible to articulate an ontological approach to the term. Still, it is certainly important that Schechner was considering performance first and foremost as an event taking place in real time. He also located the nexus away from the 'drama-script' dyad to the 'seams' (or processes) between theatre ("the specific set of gestures performed by the performers in any given performance")[4] and its realization with an audience. Similarly, he draws attention to essential differences between character-audience and performer-audience relationships, as well as the difficulty in disassociating performance from performativity (especially since, as Judith Butler has shown, performativity relies on acts of reiteration,[5] as does performance).

My concerns arise from Schechner's use of terminology, the way it is embedded in his definition of performance, and his choice of model. Although he recognizes that he

1

could have invented new words "which no one [would] pay attention to", terms like 'drama', 'script', and 'theatre' lead to a concentration on traditional theatre models or at the very least 'aesthetic genres' which involve 'theatricality and narrativity'. Setting up a model of performance which necessarily includes theatre which includes scripts which includes drama (as the model of concentric circles implies), and then admitting that these are often interchangable or non-existent is problematic. The circle does not simply work its way out; it also works its way in. The 'drama' (which Schechner at first says can be transmitted by 'messengers' who may be unable to read, comprehend or enact it, but then condenses unfortunately to "what the writer writes") is a concept which may include its performance; the 'script' may be 'written' after or during a performance; the 'theatre' may only be possible with the inclusion or collaboration of the audience. In other words, it is possible to posit a model in which drama contains script which contains theatre which contains performance. What is important here is merely that this is possible. Once the positionings of 'drama', 'script' and 'theatre' are destabilized, so is his definition of performance. His "performance magnitudes", although they can be included within a theatrical, narrative, or socially dramatic framework, largely neglect the processes outside the moments of performance. In order to define 'performance', one must consider exchanges which begin *before* the time the first spectator enters and *after* the last spectator leaves and the essence of performance resides in the fluidity of discursive processes. Schechner describes all this in practice, but his observations remain epistemological rather than ontological.

I do not mean to be unnecessarily harsh or critical of Schechner's work. The study of theatre & performance as an academic discipline is relatively young and we are still finding our feet in establishing a vocabulary by which to discuss theoretical models. Very fine consolidations such as Fortier's *Theory/Theatre* seem to avoid essential aspects of theatre practice such as creative processes and their relationship to the product *as performance*.[6] As Josette Féral has pointed out, the growing antagonism between theatre practitioners and theorists (who deal mainly with historical, sociological, or semiological aspects of performance as 'finished product'), is evidenced in the fact that there are very few examples of theorists like Schechner working today who have an impact on art and take part in its evolution.[7] The reasons for this, I believe, are (at least) twofold.

Firstly, the ephemeral 'presentness' of performance, its 'liveness', can make any attempts at retrospective analysis relying on memory seem somewhat obsolete and redundant, since even watching a mediated re-production on for example video is incomplete, or at the very least 'different', and one must (re)construct the atmosphere and feelings evoked in the course of a performance. In many ways, the 'moment' has passed and another one has already begun. The theorist is always presented with the task of catching up while the practitioner moves forward to create a concrete new 'theoretical' manifestation waiting to be articulated. Subsequently, we have begun to see theory in oppositional terms; theory has become 'not practice' rather than an essential part of practice (in the same way that dictionary definitions locate praxis as 'not theory'). It is no longer a useful framework which informs our practice, but a (re)presentation which describes and inscribes our practice. The theory becomes a performance in itself, the dialogues between 'practitioners' and 'theorists' shudder to a petulent, misunderstood, and competitive halt. It should not be this way.

Here we must distinguish between 'performance' and 'live performance' since the terms cannot be used interchangeably (although many make this assumption, perhaps due to the use of 'shorthand' when writing for a projected audience of 'theatre people'). A 'performance' in its broadest sense is the (re)presentation or documentation of a series of events which may, or may not, still be in the process of occuring. Think, for example, of performance-related pay, the financial performance of stocks and shares, the performance of building materials in the construction industry, or (most usefully in the context of this discussion) the performance of actors on film or television. A 'live performance', on the other hand, is one which is still happening and still has to happen. It includes the potential for change in its every moment of delivery through the dialectical processes which *need* to be experienced (to lesser or greater extents) – via, for example, the body of the performer, the physical context of its venue, the relationship with the audience – in order to make it 'whole'. When it is 'finished', it reverts back to (mere?) 'performance', its trace documented (even in memory) and recalled by other means.

It is for this reason that I return to Schechner again and, in particular, his idea of art as an event: an Actual. Actualization encompasses both the creative condition and the artwork itself as an organic whole, as is evident in the five basic qualities he identifies:

> 1) *process*, something happens *here and now*; 2) *consequential, irremediable,* and *irrevocable* acts, exchanges, or situations; 3) *contest*, something is *at stake* for the performers and often for the spectators; 4) *initiation*, a *change in status* for participants; 5) space is used *concretely* and *organically*.[8]

I see no reason why Schechner did not use this as a definition of 'live performance', beyond the fact that he was trying to draw distinctions between performative events and performance events. Perhaps times have simply moved on and concepts have sharpened; to me, a marriage ceremony is obviously both a ritual *and* a performance, not a ritual which is performative, and not all performance needs to include 'theatre' (as Schechner's model would seem to imply). While it is obvious that the debate over the precise meanings of these terms is far from over,[9] I would offer a slightly modified version of Butler's distinctions: while performativity can be considered the citational "reiteration of a norm or set of norms", and (live) performance can be considered a "bounded act", *both* are discursive processes. As such, I would also add to Schechner's definition of the Actual a few concepts which he articulates in other contexts in order to provide a more precise overview of the nature of 'live performance': that time is adapted to the event or else the event is organized around a consideration of time; that its production results from conscious or deliberate decisions; and that its 'text' or 'blueprint' is repeatable (although necessarily alterable when actually [re-]presented).[10]

It is perhaps Schechner's contextualizing of the Actual which problematizes its use as a definition of performance. He identifies four inseparable "yearnings" which have "triggered" an interest in this manifestation of culture: "wholeness, process and organic growth, concreteness, and religious transcendental experience".[11] His elaborations on these categories ("kicking out your feelings", "do your own thing", "dig the physicality of the experience", "freak-outs", etc.)[12], and in particular the inclusion of transcendental experience, indicate how those intimately involved with live performance invest a significance to its processes beyond its essential constituent parts. As well they should. However, when Schechner, in yet another definition in the same book, calls performance "the whole binary continuum efficacy/ritual-entertainment/theater",[13] he is confusing the ideology of live performance with its ontology.

Conflations such as these lead theorists such as Philip Auslander to declare that:

> the qualities performance theorists frequently cite to demonstrate that live performance forms are ontologically different from mediatized forms turn out, upon close examination, to provide little basis for convincing distinctions.[14]

Auslander's thesis is challenging and compelling. Situating himself against practitioner/theorists like Peggy Phelan and Eric Bogosian,[15] he argues that it is misleading to situate live performance and mediatized (or technologized) performances in opposition to each other. He shows that it is impossible to sustain theories which privilege live performance on the basis of its authenticity, reception, intimacy, or resistance to reproduction and that, due to issues of cultural economy, live performance is increasingly dominated by other types of performance with greater prestige, presence and power. According to Auslander,

> If live performance cannot be shown to be economically independent of, immune from contamination by, and ontologically different from mediatized forms, in what sense can liveness function as a site of cultural and ideological resistance...?[16]

Theories of performance which embed ideology into their construction leave themselves open to the criticism of being irrational. But while I admire Auslander's argument and agree with many of his positions, I can't help feeling that there is something missing. By defining what 'liveness' is not (that is, it is *not* "not mediatized"), he raises questions of what it *is*. I would suggest that, while Auslander is correct in destabilizing the assumption that 'live' is the opposite of 'mediatized', there *is* an ontology of liveness which allows people like Phelan to claim that "to the degree that live performance attempts to enter into the economy of reproduction it betrays and lessens the promise of its own ontology".[17] Rather than claim that live performance *is* ideologically resistant, it is more useful to suggest that the ontology of live performance somehow provides the *potential for* ideological resistance.

My suspicions were raised when reflecting on one of Auslander's illustrations, the 'live' Broadway production of Disney's *Beauty and the Beast*, which I took my daughter to see in London. Indeed, it would be difficult to claim that this grandiose and immaculately-prepared musical was 'more live' than, say, the infamously televised O.J. Simpson car chase. But, following a production number in which singing and dancing crockery and cutlery whirled impossibly through a field of pyrotechnical illusion, the audience sat in stunned silence. Then applauded. Then stood up and applauded. They were not moved emotionally or challenged intellectually by its content or even spectacular appearance (since it was a close re-production of the 'original' animation which probably did not raise lumps in the same throats), but by its 'liveness' and the potentials this includes. The ontology of this live performance was not, as Phelan suggests it should be, betrayed or lessened but highlighted and celebrated as it entered into the economy of reproduction.[18]

In order to explore this issue further, I offer the model in Figure 1 to explain what I perceive to be the nature of live performance. This cycle emphasizes five processes fundamental to the creation of performance – processes of conception, processes of development, processes of presentation, processes of reception, and processes of reflection – as well as the potentially discursive processes between them. Although I begin this list with 'conception', there is no reason to assume that all performance necessarily originates with an 'idea'; the cycle can proceed from any point (it could be argued that it never really 'begins' at all, but, rather, noticeably 'continues'). Furthermore, I have not simply substituted 'conception, development, presentation, and reception' for Schechner's 'drama, script, theatre, and performance'. There are a number of important differences: (1) we're not talking about products ('scripts',

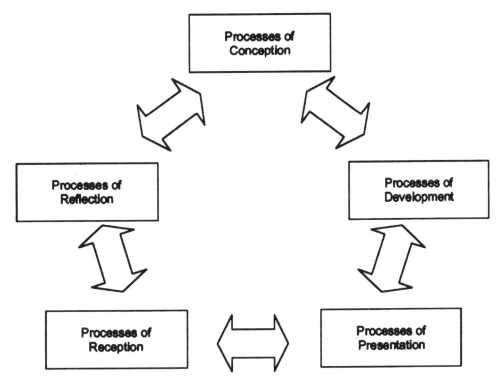

Figure 1

'dramas') but of the processes within them; (2) the relationships between these processes are processes themselves and furthermore, they are dialectical; (3) I have added the processes of reflection to indicate that these processes are cyclical and potentially never-ending. This reflection occurs both before and after the processes of conception; (4) the 'performance' itself is a manifestation of the 'processes of presentation'. In Schechner's model, it is implied that the performance did not exist before it was received. I would argue that the (live) performance only exists *as* it is received (and, even then, not necessarily by a 'traditional' audience – it could be received by other participants, the performer herself, a camera, or even possibly the 'space') and that this needs to be made explicit. It is the *potential* for discourse between the processes of presentation and the processes of preparation (which are never 'finished' until the performance is 'finished') and reception which is the defining characteristic of 'live performance'.

As such, there is no reason to suggest that 'mediatized' performances cannot be live. Some are and some are not. Mona Hatoum's two-hour long video performance, *Pull* (1995), in which viewers pulled a braid of hair and watched Hatoum's reaction on a video monitor, is undeniably live in its interactive relationship between the processes of presentation and reception. Her phenomenological responses as a performer were impossible to fully prepare before, and essential to, the presentation. Stelarc's internet performances, by exploiting the same processes, show how 'liveness' does not need to even occur in the same time, let alone space, as the audience.[19]

By way of contrast, when Neil Diamond sweated out "Girl You'll Be A Woman Soon" at the Greek Theatre in Los Angeles, it was a 'live performance'; when we listen to it at home on our eight-tracks, it is a 'performance'. This may seem obvious, but it highlights the ontology of 'liveness': it is a process which is happening in the moment, which feeds off its reception, which is 'unfinished', which always contains within it the potential to change. We can repeatedly pummel our eight-track cassette player with a hammer until we disrupt the re-presentation of Diamond's performance, but we (or he) can no longer alter the processes of the 'live' performance itself in any way (in other words, that particular 'performance' occured during a previous rotation of the cycle). The "dialectical or symbiotic relationship [is] between live and mediatized representations of the music, in which neither the recording nor the live concert could be perceived as authentic in and of itself",[20] but in the case of the recording, the dialectical relationships can no longer exist between the processes of the performer and the processes of the audience (or, perhaps more importantly, the processes of presentation and reception within the performer himself). The recording is not 'inauthentic' or even less 'original' (it is after all, a *real* and deliberate object); it is simply ontologically different.

In other words, in non-live performances the processes of preparation, presentation, and reception can only move (or influence) in a clockwise direction; in live performance, the potential always exists for the processes to be influenced either way. This is why I believe that, despite the fact that all types of performances result from the same processes, the ontology of live performance has been privileged as a site of critique in political terms.[21]

Processes of Conception

The potential for an apolitical, or at least 'neutral', ontology of performance is stressed in the opening chapter of this book. Christine Roberts' pragmatic discussion of the role of (perceived) audiences in the process of playwriting highlights the artist's negotiations between resistant and reactionary pressures. For Roberts, the solitary act of creation is necessarily mediated by the playwright's access to the means of production. These potentially stifling constraints affect the very conception and modeling of the artistic work; either the playwright second-guesses the reception of 'audiences' at every stage of a play's development (funding bodies, Artistic Directors, and critics, who each may have a different perception of future intended audiences based on commercial rather than aesthetic concerns) in order to ensure 'success', or else s/he may take the "desperate act" of setting up a new theatre company in order to perform plays to whomever, and in whatever way, s/he wishes.

The way in which issues of spectator response become intricately embedded in both the concept and delivery of live performance is also emphasized in Lorenzo Buj's overview of Iain and Ingrid Baxter's N.E. Thing Company. The Baxters' move from abstract painting to interactive installation art developed from an artistic vision which rejected commodification. These performances insisted on a "special complicity" between spectator and artist which existed in an instantaneous "moment of transcendental temporality". The performing body which follows "the Baxter method" of exploring "what happens when you try this or that", thus becomes an operative site that is neither subject or object.

Processes of Development

As such, it should not come as a suprise that so many authors in this book link the processes of conception and development to performance events which need to be understood phenomenologically. "Higher than actuality stands *possibility*," wrote Martin Heidegger, "The comprehension of phenomenology consists solely in grasping it as possibility".[22] According to Ruth Way, choreographic processes like Yolande Snaith's which focus on collaboration, improvisation and performer ownership, produce "thinking bodies" which reject conscious control and embrace contradictions. The act of watching such performances thereby is transformed into the act of witnessing; audience members must respond to kinesthetic, aural, somatic, spatial and emotional sensations as thinking bodies like the performers.

The embodiment of creative processes in the performance work of poets is fundamental to Tony Lopez's analysis of both his own practice and the context in which it is situated. Echoing Way's phenomenal dancer, the poet who conceives of his/her writing as performance "must surrender control because what happens happens in real time, with all the unexpected contingencies that could meet a site-specific improvisation for a particular audience". The performance itself becomes the moment of composition rather than a 'definitive' and formal interpretation of a given text.

Processes of Presentation

It would be convenient to claim that the ordering of the chapters in this book was based on a transparent progression from processes of conception through to processes of reflection. This of course would be impossible given the discursive nature of these processes; one could literally begin at any point in the cycle. However, as a general rule, I have placed chapters which deal more specifically with the active role of the spectator towards the latter half of the book. Robert Cheesmond's discussion of the collaboration between audience and performer in English pantomime shows how the development of the performance is often literally incomplete without the participation of the spectator.[23] The audience is 'receiving', 'reflecting' and responding (performing), often through intertextual considerations, and the performer (and his/her character) must process this in kind. Both performer and spectator tread an unstable path which straddles actuality and illusion, the "visible" and the "hidden", the "actual" and the "virtual", through a shared understanding of unwritten conventions.[24]

Whereas most of the performance 'products' discussed in this book have been essentially shaped by their processes of development, Ruru Li and David Jiang explore how, in the case of *jingju* (or Peking Opera as it is known in the West), the methods of development (training, rehearsal, composition) and later reception are primarily informed by the style of performance. Conventionalization, or specific patterns and rules which practitioners must follow, is an aesthetic principle which guides all aspects of the performer's presentation, scenography, and spectator/actor relationship. This over-arching aesthetic concept enters into a dialogue with its ideological implications, and the performance becomes a process of balancing the innovative with the traditional. Just as Ruru Li consulted her mother, actress Li Yuru, in the writing of this chapter, audiences must learn how to receive *jingju* performance through the phenomenon of internalized authority. According to Eugenio Barba, "What is of short duration is not theatre, but performance. Theatre is made of traditions, conventions, institutions, habits which are permanent in time".[25]

Processes of Reception

Semiotic approaches have a tendency to remain linear; even Pavis's 'hourglass' model requires turning over before processes 'begin' again. The semiotic processes of encoding, de-coding, and re-encoding as described by Aston and Savona,[26] imply a reductibility that can focus a given performance to a core (correct) essence rather than a sum total of conflicting experiences. Ellie Parker illustrates how, in the absence of conventionally understood and accepted meaning(s), the artist's intent and the spectator's perception can vary wildly. In the simplified and probably glib model used by so many of us, performance is considered the meeting point(s) of performer, spectator and space. The critic becomes the privileged Everyspectator who validates the ephemeral live performance through documentation. The published review reflects the performance back to its makers and also projects this reflection into public currency. It is no wonder so many contributors to this volume cite examples of critics who "miss the point" and complain that the lack of education/empathy amongst critics (as surrogate spectators) jeopardizes the future of live performance. If the artists seem ambiguous, their work open to a multiplicity of mis-understandings (perhaps intentionally and this too is misunderstood) and 'wrong' responses, then for the artists the critics are also providing too little to build upon. Their reflections stop the processional circle in its tracks.

Henry Daniel examines some of the difficulties artists and spectators alike face when dealing with movement-based performance and new media technologies. He proposes that this performance genre cannot wholly rely on previously established methodologies to fully explain its processes; there is a need for new approaches developed by performers themselves that can address some of the specific problems that arise from creative interactions with these technologies. In reaffirming the idea that the creative process lies as much in the actions of the performer and the perceiver/spectator as in the environment itself, Daniel uses the concept of corporeal re-cognition to identify and deal with those feelings of 'otherness' that are the inevitable result of working with 'sensitive' and 'intelligent' electronic systems.

Processes of Reflection

Kevin Winkler draws attention to the inter-connectedness between processes of reflection and processes of conception in his chapter on Bette Midler which is also about the recuperation of 'otherness'. When Midler began her career at the Continental Baths, she quickly recognized that the conventions of other nightclubs and cabarets were inappropriate. The Continental's unorthodox performance space, the near-nudity of the all-male audience, and the fact that live entertainment functioned as an adjunct to the baths' primary purpose (to provide a setting for sex) forced Midler to conceive a highly flamboyant and outrageous act. She therefore began the process of refining and embellishing camp elements which, in collaboration with her audience, created a new form of cabaret that gave gay sensibilities a broader expression. Midler's identification with her audience also meant that she was well placed to reflect the community's new sense of liberation and self-respect, both as a celebration within the gay rights movement and, later, to the mainstream.

These processes of identification and reflection are also present in every chapter of this book, since the contributors are all practitioners themselves. The way in which they are attempting to articulate and analyze the practice of others is not only informed by their own creative experiences, but is almost certainly also a way of reflecting on their own practices. This is perhaps nowhere more evident than in Ruth Way's illuminating and confident conversation with Yolande Snaith, as one choreographer/performer to another speaking with the same vocabulary. Theory here is not conscientious collection (a 're-search') but conscious creative process (a 'search').

Karen Malpede's comparison of her own work with that of dissident Croatian playwright Slobodan Snajder illustrates how practice and theory can merge into praxis by highlighting a full rotation of the cycle from conception to reflection. A shocking empathic experience set it in motion: "something inside touches something outside, the sparks ignite, then one can begin to write". Her approach to writing, rehearsing, and experiencing performance develops from, and mirrors, crises such as these. This 'theatre of witness' affects and stimulates the playwright, the actors and ultimately the audience as they each pass through ordeals which alter their understandings of personal memory:

> By putting the witnessing action and its crises before us, alive in time in space, the theatre of witness provides its audience with the knowledge, the courage, the time, and the community in which to contemplate and affirm its engagement in actual, private and public acts of witness.

For Malpede, like many other artists discussed here, it is the ontology of 'liveness' which allows for ideological resistance. She has recently been making theatre with survivors of human rights abuse in Chile. Following Malpede's identification with other artists like Snajder and reflections and consolidations of her ideas in writing such as this, the 'theory' becomes more focused and clearly developed in her practice.

The chapters in this book explore the relationship between the processes of creating performance and the processes of its presentation and reception, which usually includes spectator response. The authors show how process is embedded into the product itself and how this dynamic always potentially embodies an exchange between those who make performance and their intended audiences. The contents are not expected to comprehensively discuss all types of performance or the elements contained within them; they are meant to provide specific examples from which to draw an overarching theory of how process, performance product and reception are fused and why it is impossible to delineate discrete theoretical borders when investigating live performance.

Acknowledgements

Thank you to each of the contributors to this volume, many of whom are not only colleagues and collaborators, but also friends. This book has also been made possible by the many colleagues at the University of Plymouth who have offered ideas, support and opportunities, as well as by p.p., who considers discussions about ontology and phenomenology sexy.

Notes

1   Anthony Frost & Ralph Yarrow, *Improvisation in Drama* (Basingstoke: Macmillan,1990), p. 79.

2   Richard Schechner, *Performance Theory* (New York & London: Routledge, 1988), p. 85.

3   *ibid.*, p. 72.

4   *ibid.*, p. 85.

5   Judith Butler, *Bodies That Matter: On the Discursive Limits of 'Sex'* (London: Routledge, 1993).

6   Mark Fortier, *Theory/Theatre: an introduction* (London: Routledge, 1997).

7   Josette Féral, 'Theory and Practice: Bridging the Gap', conference paper delivered at the FIRT/IFTR XIII World Congress, Canterbury U.K, July 1998.

8   Schechner, *op. cit.*, p. 51.

9   See Geraldine Harris, *Staging Femininities: performance and performativity* (Manchester & New York: Manchester University Press, 1999), pp. 72-81.

10 I realize that this brings up some contentious issues. However, I would suggest that all live performances (or, at least, their processes of presentation) need to 'begin' and 'end' at identifiable times, even if these are not arranged in advance or necessarily recognized when they occur; that somebody has chosen to create the performance within its context (so a 'performance' of trained seals at an aquarium may not result from the conscious decisions of the seals themselves, but it is considered a deliberate event by the organizers); and that the ideology or purpose of the performance *may* change in its re-presentation (I acknowledge that, although the above-mentioned marriage ceremony *can* be repeated, it does not have the same legal, emotional, or social functions). It is also important to note here that, despite appearances, the purpose of this introduction is to provide an inclusive rather than exclusive definition of live performance, while establishing some of its boundaries, in order to explore the nature of the processes which contribute to its ontology.

11 Schechner, *op. cit.*, p. 39-40.

12 It should be noted that Schechner's essay was originally published in 1970.

13 *ibid.*, p. 141-2.

14 Philip Auslander, *Liveness: Performance in a Mediatized Culture* (London: Routledge, 1999), p. 159.

15 See Peggy Phelan, *Unmarked: The Politics of Performance* (London: Routledge, 1993) and Eric Bogosian, *Pounding Nails in the Floor With My Forehead* (New York: Theatre Communication Group, 1994). Here I feel it is apt to point out that I realize the use of Schechner's theories as the starting point of this introduction is rather old-fashioned by now. However, his ideas are still the first port of call for many students of theatre and performance. And also, I do not feel it is worth denying the origins of my own views articulated here. My reflections on Schechner's models are integral to the processes of my own conception, development and presentation of 'theoretical performance'.

16 Auslander, *op. cit.*, p. 7.

17 Phelan, *op. cit.*, p. 146.

18 I am reminded here of another example which contributed to my interrogation of 'liveness'. I once read a Sunday supplement article about the performers in character costumes at Disney World (known as "cast members") who are (allegedly) forbidden from appearing in partial costume in front of the public, in order to maintain the carefully-preserved illusionistic environment. Using Auslander's terminology, these "franchised performances" function as "templates" as each character must be generated from a single interpretation (pp. 49-50). However, despite the Disney Corporation's most authoritarian attempts, the 'liveness' of the performances can never be completely suppressed. One disgruntled ex-employee described how actors became ill and were prohibited from removing their costumes. Apparently, when temperatures rise and actors pass out from the heat in their costumes, close observers of the Main Street parade occasionally notice vomit dribbling out of Goofy's nose. Even Disney can't guarantee that the transparency of processes between character and performer is fully erased when 'live'.

19 I realize that this appears to be at odds with my advocating the use of Schechner's description of the Actual to help define performance. It is perhaps the concept of 'space' which has most destabilized our working definitions of performance since the development of new technologies. While it is certainly difficult to conceive of a 'concrete' use of cyber-space, it is still possible to posit an organic use of shared space which is appropriate to the live medium as a fundamental element of performance practice.

20 Auslander, *op. cit.*, p. 160.

21 *ibid.*, p. 43.

22 Martin Heidegger, 'My Way to Phenomenology', trans. Joan Stambaugh, in Walter Kaufman (ed), *Existentialism from Dostoevsky to Sartre* (New York: Meridian, 1975), p. 241.

23 "Oh yes it is."

24 Schechner uses the latter two pairings when discussing the relationship between social and aesthetic drama (*op. cit.*, pp. 190 - 191). He cites Victor Turner: "Human beings learn through experience ... and perhaps the deepest experience is through drama; not through social drama, or stage drama (or its equivalent) alone but in the circulatory or oscillatory process of their mutual and incessant modification." It is a viewpoint enforced by every author in this book.

25 Cited in Patrice Pavis, *Theatre at the Crossroads of Culture*, trans. Loren Kruger (London & New York: Routledge, 1992), p. 12. Pavis's hourglass (p. 4) provides a useful semiotic model for understanding the production and reception of performance, particularly in the case of Li & Jiang's discussion of *jingju* (though, of course, in the context of this chapter, source and target cultures are usually assumed to be the same thus resulting in intra- rather than inter-cultural readings of the implications). For most of the illustrations in this book however, Pavis's hourglass could best be considered a meta-model; the processes involved in the production of an individual's performance work mirror the dialectical and symbiotic relationships between performance as cultural product and culture itself.

26 Elaine Aston & George Savona, *Theatre as Sign-System: A Semiotics of Text and Performance* (London & New York: Routledge, 1991), p. 142.

1 Desperate Acts
The Role of the Audience in the Process of Playwriting

Christine Roberts

Introduction

With the exception of a small group of playwrights who create their plays through workshopping techniques, most playwrights engage in this process of creation as a solitary act. Who then is the playwright writing for? Is s/he writing with a particular audience in mind or is the play driven by an exploration of themes and ideas which are then deemed more suited to a particular audience? Does the playwright write as a literary exercise or is the notion of its performative aspects taken into account at the time of writing? To a certain extent the answer to these questions clearly depends on the individual playwright, but the decisions made by a playwright are mediated by his/her access to the means of the production of these plays.

Theatre is a live, interactive medium so although plays are clearly written texts, in my opinion they should be written to be performed. It is here the first complication in the notion of audience occurs. For a play to be performed it usually means an acceptance of that play by an established theatre or theatre company. The Artistic Director of a theatre is driven not only by aesthetic concerns but also commercial ones. His or her (and as we will see later in this chapter, it is usually his) concept of audience may differ greatly from the playwright's. If his main consideration is to ensure a commercial success then clearly he will be looking for a particular type of play which will guarantee this. What of the playwright who is tackling themes which may not be considered 'mainstream'? Or is writing in a style which is not easily classifiable? What happens to these texts? In this chapter I aim to explore the variety of ways in which playwrights generally, and female playwrights in particular, overcome this second perception of the concept of audience; and why, despite their considerable success as writers they continue to be under-represented in mainstream theatre. As Lizbeth Goodman points out, if 'serious' theatre is safeguarded by men who regard women as the exception, then as they come under increasing threat from financial cut-backs and decreasing funds they revert towards safer territory.

> There is a desire to see theatre as a place that is all about taking risks, as a place that is about experiment and not stasis. But clearly theatre is a place that allows for certain types of chance-taking and not others; it is possible for theatre to be a world that pushes boundaries, but leaves some intact.[1]

I would maintain this happens for reasons not only linked to those of gender but also because of particular themes and styles adopted by playwrights of both sexes. So, how many of these considerations is the playwright aware of during the act of writing a play? Indeed, how many of these *should* the playwright be aware of when writing? What happens during this process?

The Act of Writing

The most basic of questions has to be, does the text of a play stand as a literary piece of writing? If so, the writer is writing with one audience in mind – the reader – who then becomes responsible for imaginatively providing additional information such as gesture, movement, use of time and space, etc. If, however, we accept Raymond Williams' notion that "the text does no more than prescribe an *effect*, of which the *means* must be worked out performance"[2], the writer's relationship with both his/her audience and the actual written text is a much more complex one.

Playwright Sarah Daniels describes this process of writing for theatre as getting harder, not easier, the more she becomes aware of its complexities. She cites Bryony Lavery as describing it as "a big nutty fruit cake made up of the script, the director, the designer, actors, technicians and audience"[3]. Daniels continues to explain that when it works, it does so because everyone has invested talent and passion in it. A brilliant script, she suggests, does not necessarily make a brilliant play. Similarly, a dull script can 'glow' with brilliant direction, design and acting:

> The playwright has to learn to 'let go' to enable the process to happen. There will always be things in a production which were not how I saw them in my head. The skills and imagination which directors and actors bring can enhance a play greatly. (Although, I am sometimes left feeling like a big nutty fruit cake all on my own and, at the risk of sounding sensational, however dangerously on the edge of wanting to shout, 'No, I didn't mean it like that at all').[4]

Derrida's explanation of how theatricality is deferred is useful here. He explains that the dramatic component is encoded "in the writing itself: the clause structures, for example remain stable, as does the order of speech – but other aspects are differently coded, between dramatic writing (always in writing for theatre) and the context-specific conditions of actualisation".[5]

Not all writers are so philosophical about letting their work go however. Arnold Wesker states in his seminar paper 'Playing with the writer's rights' that "when I go to a theatre it is the author's voice, his or her perceptions ... that I want to hear, not the actress's". He continues:

> if the director is imposing his views in a stage production by cutting text, re-arranging the sequence of events, placing the action in a setting different from what the author has imagined: and if the actress is interpreting the unfaithful wife as a ruthless woman, then how will you know what it was that the author wanted to say?[6]

He also makes the case that given the many opportunities for mis-representation in the theatre, many directors are now writing their own plays, many actresses directing their own performances and many writers 'sculpting their own work'.

No matter how much a writer wishes to control the interpretation of her/his work when writing for production s/he must be prepared for the encoding and decoding of the text which take place at many different levels. These stages are clearly indicated in Aston and Savona's *Theatre as Sign System*. They set them out as follows in four stages:

- The dramatist encodes the text in terms of her/his perception of its function as a blueprint for theatrical production.
- The director decodes the text, initiates a process of commission or collaboration with a production team and arrives at a *mise-en-scene.*
- The designer re-encodes the text to develop a portfolio of designs, within a pre-determined or negotiated brief and subject to interpretative, spatial and budgetary constraints.
- The spectator decodes the production, works upon and is worked upon by the visual dimension as an integral aspect of the reception process.[7]

From the playwright's perspective the important point here is the awareness that the writing is a 'blueprint for production'. A playtext may stand on its own as an outstanding piece of literary text (Shakespeare and Beckett bear testament to this), but essentially a playwright writes texts to be physically realized. This factor alone dictates viewing not only the prospective audience differently, but the very act of writing. The objective is to construct an informed performance text.

As Aston and Savona point out, the concept of time (present, chronological, plot, and performance) is an important consideration when constructing a text for performance.[8] How time is used in the text is dependent on the style and intentions of the writer; how it is interpreted in performance is largely dependent on the director and actors. But this consideration alone dictates a very different process of creation. The very use of the word text also needs to be considered in that two very different forms of dialogue are employed. Ingarden employs the terms *Haupttext* ('primary text') and *Nebentext* ('ancillary text') to differentiate between the dialogue of the characters and the stage directions which frame that dialogue.[9] In performance the spoken word may not always be paramount; theatre is essentially symbolic and other visual or aural elements may acquire equal if not more importance. Similarly the role of stage directions varies in importance depending on both the individual writer and the style of performance. Some writers consider them important not only to give added information but also as an attempt to retain some autonomy over their work. They can also be viewed in more creative terms when the primary text of dialogue gives way to physical or visual dimensions of the performance. Essentially they provide a starting point for those involved in the production of the piece but once in production, they can also be totally disregarded.

The director Deborah Warner failed to realise the authority of Beckett's stage directions and, in choosing to disregard them in 1994 when directing *Footfalls* at the

Garrick Theatre, brought the wrath of the Beckett Estate on her head. As a result the production was abruptly terminated and she has since been banned from producing any of his work. These are general considerations; obviously emphasis is placed according to the individual playwright. Sarah Daniels believes that style is often given more credence than content. To her the importance of the writing is paramount:

> I'm afraid I'm old fashioned enough to think, I don't care how beautiful, ritzy, glitzy, dazzly or weird anything looks, I want to be intellectually and emotionally involved in it. I want to engage with it on a gut level.[10]

Whereas Debbie Isitt, having trained as an actor, places emphasis on the role of the actor in creating the relationship between audience and play:

> Without the actor's influence, correct interpretation, creativity, contribution, the dramatic experience wouldn't exist. That's how the art form of theatre works.[11]

She would certainly be supported by the actor Peter O'Toole who in a recent article in *The Observer* (11 July 1999), cited the rise of the director's role, as personified by Trevor Nunn and Peter Hall, as one of the main reasons he has given up theatre-acting. He saw their role as interpreters of text as an affront to the professional actor who had been trained and had honed his craft. Ironically O'Toole's long-standing friend Richard Burton held a very different view. He was outspoken in his condemnation of the profession of acting, seeing it as a mindless activity, referring to the writer as the only creative person in the process.[12]

Structure, for Phylis Nagy, is the major influence on her writing. She states that, "I actually think that plays are structured the way certain forms of music are structured.... I couldn't write anything without bearing in mind the principles of musical composition".[13] She is also very sceptical when writers explain how in the process of writing "the character took over" and suddenly the play was "writing itself". "It isn't some mystical process," she says, "whereby no one knows what they're doing.... We're not mediums."[14]

Helen Edmundson writes very much with the actor in mind, to the point that her texts have been accused of 'looking slightly odd'. She believes that knowing how an actor acts means she can cut the words back:

> I do that naturally and I do it even more when we get into rehearsal. They'll be playing a scene and I'll think, 'That's just so obvious. He really doesn't need to say it because he's doing it'.[15]

Without losing sight of the power of the written word, some playwrights write with a very clear visualization of images and how they will work physically and symbolically on stage. Symbolism happens when elements become more significant than their tangible meanings, and this is why, when effectively harnessed, theatre becomes such a powerful resonator of meaning. It is obvious that as a playwright you cannot predict how an audience will respond or control how it reacts, but as Sarah Kane commented, "You have to know what you want to do to them. What I think about when I'm writing is how I want it to affect me and the best way to achieve that".[16]

Clearly the 'best way to achieve that' will depend on the individual writer's personal perspective. Although the writing of a playtext for performance involves a difficult and complex process, in many ways I feel the real difficulties occur after the play has been written. At the time of writing autonomy generally resides with the writer. But not for long. As Jenny McLeod states, "playwriting is a process where you pass it on".[17] So if you want your plays to be performed (and if you write plays, why wouldn't you?), the next realisation, as pointed out by Winsome Pinnock, is that as a writer you are dependent on individuals to make it happen. "It doesn't matter how much you write, it has no power if people don't allow it to be heard".[18]

So what are the factors which dictate whether your work is heard or not? This question involves the exploration of a wide range of people, institutions, social and cultural factors. They are diverse in their motivations and powerful in their influences.

Constraining Factors

Throughout this section I will be examining five areas which can be seen as having a constraining effect on the production and promotion of playtexts. At times these interrelate, but I will attempt to give a focused analysis of the individual areas and the extent of their influence on the production of both the play and the playtext.

Gender

Many of the issues explored in this section apply equally to both men and women playwrights. But I feel given Jennie Long's survey *What Share of the Cake Now?*, a more focused analysis of the particular difficulties facing female playwrights is needed. This survey was the follow-up survey to one commissioned by the Womens' Playhouse Trust in 1985/6 which looked at patterns of employment and the status of women in English theatre companies in receipt of Arts Council revenue grants. Entitled *What Share of the Cake?*, it found that whilst there had been some positive developments in the position of women in the theatre, they were still proportionately under-represented. Jennie Long's survey was carried out in 1993/4 and, at the moment, gives the most up-to-date picture of the current situation for women involved in all aspects of the theatre. One of the most disturbing figures relates to the production of plays by women. In most cases, the numbers have actually decreased since the 1985/6 report:

> Productions written, devised or adapted by women, or from books by women, account for only 20% of all work performed in 1994. In 1985/6 the figure had been 22%. Out of the 417 plays produced during 1994 (this involves not only building-based theatres but also touring companies and annual clients) only 83 were by women.[19]

The under-representation not only occurs on the stage or in performance, but also in print.

Charlotte Keatley reports a recent meeting with the critic Michael Billington, who sees himself as a great supporter of new writing. He has recently published a book of collected reviews from his years as a theatre critic:

> I think *Serious Money* and *Light Shining in Buckinghamshire* (both by Caryl Churchill) are the only plays by a living woman in the whole collection.... [A] book like that says to other people 'The theatre has been constructed by men, directed by men.... These are the milestones. These are the representatives of our society'.[20]

Theatre managements often maintain that women do not currently submit the number of plays that men do. Graham Wybrow, the Royal Court's literary manager, says that out of a sample batch of scripts he looked at recently, only 189 out of one thousand were by women. "This necessarily means that the ratio of work selected by them will be lower".[21] Jenny Topper, Artistic Director at Hampstead Theatre makes the same point. But as Stephenson and Langridge acknowledge, number-crunching both is, and is not, at the heart of the matter:

> The responsibility lies with theatres too. The theatre establishment expends little energy, in real terms, to welcome new women writers into the theatre or to value the more established playwrights. What would inspire fledgling dramatists to submit plays when they see the work of good, experienced female dramatists frequently being undermined and undervalued, not only by critics, but by theatre practitioners themselves? It's a self-fulfilling prophecy.[22]

When we consider that not one play by a living female playwright has ever made it to the main Olivier Stage at the National (the closest Caryl Churchill got was the medium-sized Lyttleton), or that the four plays showcasing the Royal Court's Young Writers Festival in December 1998 were written exclusively by men, the situation looks bleak.

As Long reported in her survey, "this section [productions by women] has produced one of the bleakest scenarios of the whole survey, and the findings of greatest concern".[23] She highlights not only the overall trend but points out that companies where the Artistic Director is male stage much less work by women than companies where the Artistic Director is female. Given the fact that in 1985, 34% of Artistic Directors were women, but in Long's survey of 1994 that percentage had dropped to 28%, there seems little hope of changes coming about in that direction. Stephen Daldry, the outgoing Artistic Director of the Royal Court was keen to point out that:

> Statistically speaking the Royal Court in the last three years has produced more women playwrights than ever in its history, but that the figures are somewhat distorted because the Royal Court is also now producing more new plays than ever before.... No. We don't put on enough women.[24]

This situation is further complicated by the range of people involved in the production of a play.

As stated earlier in the chapter, there are many mediating factors which have to be considered when a play is chosen for production. As Jack Bradley, formerly with the Soho Theatre Company and now literary manager at the Royal National Theatre, points out, it doesn't matter how enthusiastic his department gets about a play, if there's no director behind it, the likelihood is that it won't go on. This problem is aggravated by the fact that women directors frequently choose to stage the work of male playwrights or go with the classics.[25] This would certainly seem to be borne out in an article on the Royal Shakespeare Company in which the director Kate Mitchell admits she prefers her authors to be dead, "deader even than Lorca", who died in 1936, "and Hauptmann", who died in 1946.[26] Her choice of plays for that particular season (1997) also revealed that not only were the playwrights mostly dead, they were also all male. So what of Mitchell's influence on the male-dominated society?

The question which now has to be raised is why? From the research available it certainly seems harder for women playwrights to get their work produced. Is this a conscious attempt to keep women out of the theatre? I think one of the answers is even more straightforward than that. "Commercial considerations," admits Richard Eyre, "also come into the equation; raising the question of whether theatres perhaps view the work of women playwrights as more of a commercial risk".[27]

Finance

The financial climate will obviously effect non-established playwrights of both sexes. But where women are so obviously under-represented it must be another major obstacle in getting work produced. Figures of Arts Council funding produced in February 1999 revealed that 55% small and mid-scale companies are on standstill funding. For many of them it is for the fifth or sixth year. At the other end of the scale the big companies emerged as headline winners. The Royal National Theatre received a 9% increase, worth £1 million per year, the Royal Shakespeare Company 5% to bring its annual subsidy to £8.9 million. As Nicola Thorold, director of the Independent Theatre Council states, "The Arts Council says this is a radical budget but it's a nonsense. They've shifted the money to a few by keeping the small companies on standstill".[28] The recent funding situation and the New Labour party's apparent lack of support has led Sir Peter Hall to leave England to work in America. He stated in a recent article in *The Guardian* that "Art and market forces never mix. Art is necessarily innovative, unexpected and frequently unpopular".[29] He develops this in Glaister's article adding that, "The way in which regional theatres are funded will lead to their disappearance. We will have one or two centres, say Leeds and Birmingham. The small houses where audiences learn how to be audiences are disappearing".[30]

This notion of audiences learning to be audiences is an interesting and important one. As audiences become more familiar with a wide range of plays both in terms of style and content, their critical faculties will obviously be enhanced. The more you see and the more diverse the diet, the more you will be able to appreciate. The current situation for small and regional companies is, according to Terry Hands, once Artistic

Director of the Royal Shakespeare Company and now of Clwyd Theatr Cymru, "at its lowest point since the 19th century".[31] The National Campaign for the Arts (NCA) gave figures showing a £12m loss for regional theatres over the past ten years; 33 English rep theatres have deficits totalling £10.3m; ticket prices have risen more than 90% in a decade.[32]

The situation, where to run any kind of risk could close your theatre or company or at least the run of the show, is generally solved by serving up a diet of well-worn, tried and tested plays. This has an adverse effect on new playwrights, playwrights writing in a challenging style or about controversial themes, and, as Peter Hall stated, ultimately does a disservice to the audience. Audiences become so used to the bland diet they receive that anything a little more spicy gives them indigestion. Sally Hughes, Artistic Director of The Mill near Reading, states that they are able to fill their houses every Saturday night by providing a dramatic fare not selected to challenge: "Nothing too shocking – they don't mind a bit of nudity, but we wouldn't do *Shopping and Fucking* for instance – nothing too political".[33] Sadly this is a picture reflected all over the country and basically it boils down to the fact that, as John Newman, Artistic Director for Newpalm Productions a resident company at Chelmsford's Civic Theatre states, "Subsidy is a two-edged sword. It's a nice cushion, but you always run the risk of losing it if you don't programme the way someone else wants you to do it. We don't go into the artistic elite".[34]

The effect of these factors on what is actually written by playwrights is immense. Would it be too simple to say that you either write to a trend, to a fashion, and have a chance of being produced, or write what you feel you have to, in the style which best suits your themes, but fail to get your work accepted?

Styles and Themes

The current batch of new plays being produced certainly seems to be following a particular trend. My own observations about this are supported by other playwrights. Pam Gems notes that although the Royal Court is doing some interesting new work, not much of it is by women, "and it's mostly all this pseudo-butch stuff: the alienated urban creature – doing what America did ten years ago. All they want to be is Quentin Tarantino or Bruce Willis".[35] This view is repeated by Charlotte Keatley in the same book when she states that, "The current vogue for American film criteria quite alarms me. All the plays seem to be called 'Sex and Violence' or something close to that". She continues:

> Plays like *Mojo*. Yes, so Jez Butterworth can write great, wacky dialogue, but it's yet again another play about a bunch of men doing nothing much. I'm glad he's found success, but it does piss you off that there's this endless lineage, going back through the centuries, of men writing plays about men doing nothing much.[36]

It is interesting to note that the obvious exception to this trend for American-styled theatre is the successful play by Conor McPherson called *The Weir*. This was produced by the Royal Court and began life originally as a radio play. It is Irish and clearly not driven by a need to replicate Tarantino, but still fits quite neatly into Keatley's description of themes.

The drive by Artistic Directors to always produce a success, both because of reputation and financial considerations, can also have a stifling effect on new or innovative writing. If there is a given formula of work which will be successful (be it Alan Ayckbourne in Scarborough or Mark Ravenhill in London), are new plays considered with this blueprint in the reader's mind? Would the corollary then be that playwrights are tempted to write to this formula in desperation to have their work accepted? Sarah Daniels comments that she feels there is too much emphasis on the new play having to be a success.

> When I first started writing people put on plays they believed in. Nobody talked about box-office. That's changed now because theatres have to consider how best to keep afloat, even subsidised theatres. But if they won't take risks, who will? ... [W]here are the new plays, the second and third plays by writers?[37]

Due to financial considerations involved in employing a large cast, playwrights are advised to tailor their plays to include no more than four actors; and as we have seen from Long's survey, new plays, and particularly plays by women are more often performed in studio spaces than main houses. These sound like logistical considerations, but both will have an increasing effect on what is actually being written and the style in which it can be performed. Playwrights like Timberlake Wertenbaker who write for large casts are now in the minority.

The style in which a play is written can also be a contributing factor in its progress into production. If you want your play to be accepted should you write it according to the Mill's criteria of 'nothing too shocking'? Or, when you realize that if you are produced it will probably be in a small black box of studio space, should you adapt your style accordingly? And what of the critics? How do they affect the writer? The complexities and dilemmas facing the playwright become clearer and more daunting as this vast range of considerations and 'audiences' are highlighted. However, I feel I have to agree with the late Sarah Kane when she stated:

> My only responsibility as a writer is to the truth, however unpleasant that truth may be. I have no responsibility as a woman writer because I don't believe there's such a thing. When people talk about me as a writer, that's what I am, and that's how I want my work to be judged – on its quality, not on the basis of my age, gender, class, sexuality or race. I am what I am. Not what other people want me to be.[38]

Amen sister!

This unequivocal statement of intention seems uncompromising and each individual writer has to decide how far s/he is willing to compromise her/his work to gain access to production. Or, as in Kane's case, be ready for the wrath of The Critics.

Critics

As Stephenson and Langridge discovered in their interviews with a range of female playwrights, critics come under considerable attack. "In an age where a playwright's success is largely measured by critical approval and closely linked to this, how well they do at the box-office, critics wield huge power".[39] Phylis Nagy believes that because critics are conditioned to watch only a certain kind of play [of the exposition, crisis, resolution order] when they see something unfamiliar and they fail to understand it, they attack.[40] This view is supported by Claire Armistead, Arts Editor of *The Guardian*. She believes that critics still take their benchmark from *Look Back in Anger* (first performed in 1956):

> As a critic it's very intimidating when the work you are reviewing fundamentally challenges the very precepts by which you write: linguistic, logical, linear narrative structures. That can lead you to a defensive reaction which says, 'This is not theatre'.[41]

I feel when a writer writes with the main intention of being produced or accepted by either the critics (if that can ever be predicted) or a target audience, rather than from the desire to communicate ideas or beliefs, the activity becomes cynically commercial. This is not to suggest that all writers who are successful compromise their work; and it also has to be acknowledged that however worthy one's beliefs and ideas are, if as already stated, you are not produced, these views are not heard.

There are recognised outlets which encourage new and innovative work, such as the Soho Theatre Company, the Bush, BAC, the new Ambassador's Theatre and these need to be commended. But they cannot cater for all the country. What happens to those writers/directors/theatre-makers who feel they are not accommodated within the mainstream? They do one of two things: (1) they give up, and this is threatened not just by 'unknowns'. Phylis Nagy has recently stated that:

> If things carry on the way they are currently, with this 'laddism', this ridiculous promotion of men and bad plays and misogyny, then I, for one, will stop writing plays. I will no longer be a playwright in that sort of theatre culture. I will find something else to do instead.[42]

Or, (2) they take the desperate act of finding alternative routes and doing it themselves. I call this a desperate act because, if the roles of finance, the critics, and the audience is important in mainstream theatre, they are absolutely vital on the fringe.

Alternative Routes

This is not merely the route for a few unknown women becoming disenchanted and bitter after receiving constant rejections from the large or not-so-large nationals. Many famous playwrights and theatre-makers have been forced to follow this route, either because their themes were considered too contentious or they wanted to explore more experimental styles of performance; they wanted to reach different audiences. Two notable people who have chosen this route are in fact men, Steven Berkoff and Howard

Barker, both of whom have chosen or felt compelled to set up their own theatre companies and tour the regional theatres or work the fringe and theatre pub circuit.

The Wrestling School was established in 1988 by Kenny Ireland to act as a focus for the work of Howard Barker, "whose distinctive and metaphorical style of theatre required the development of new techniques of presentation in both performance and design".[43] Not only do they perform Barker's work, but he has become increasingly involved in writing for and directing them. At a post-performance discussion of his latest play, *Und*, Barker admitted that it was unlikely that he would have his work performed at theatres such as the National. He explained that he realised if he wanted to produce the kind of work he felt was important to the theatre he would have to do it himself. The company has presented fourteen productions, numerous workshops, readings and public discussions, "to over 63,000 people in eleven countries". So despite what mainstream Artistic Directors may say, there is obviously an audience out there waiting, and probably very eager, for this type of theatre.

Similarly, Steven Berkoff became disenchanted with his career in mainstream theatre, describing it like being a lottery ticket-holder waiting for his number to come up:

> I wanted to exercise the possibility of an actor being stretched beyond the pale of naturalism and to create theatre that was truly theatrical, that penetrated beneath the surface of human activity with its simple human conflicts and ego-bound convention that obsesses most playwrights. [Kafka's *Metamorphosis*] allowed me the scope to explore, experiment and extend my vision and, finally, to be responsible for my own creation.[44]

Both Barker and Berkoff have been successful in their ventures and both continue to work small theatres, theatre pubs and fringe establishments. Both have also been acknowledged by the mainstream theatre for their innovative styles.

Debbie Isitt cites Berkoff as one of her initial inspirations, particularly his play *East*. Isitt is one of many playwrights, actors or directors who have chosen more experimental ways of working. She joined Cambridge Experimental Theatre Company because she wanted to find a new way of making her work both accessible and at the same time find a new style or form. She admits to the incredible difficulties facing anyone taking this route:

> It's very easy to allow this industry to silence you. You know, you can't get on in the right theatre, your play can't be put in the right theatre, you won't be seen. How do you overcome that? ... That's the challenge. How do you keep growing as an artist and yet keep fighting the system? It's a constant battle. I intend to stay with it.[45]

Many artists form their own companies because they feel it is the only way their work will be produced, whilst others make the conscious decision to opt out of the mainstream to work in a more egalitarian way.

Commercial theatre is characterised by hierarchical structures and limited, prescriptive rehearsal schedules as dictated by lack of time and financial concerns. This process can disempower playwright and actor alike. Alternatives can allow for a greater input by all the company, ensemble styles of work permit the possibilities of devising and adapting scripts and experimentation with styles and forms. Many playwrights choose to direct their own work as a means of protecting it, whilst others prefer to work in a collaborative way with a specific director or within the ensemble (Caryl Churchill began her theatre career in this way). There are immense benefits to starting your own production company. Setting up your own company permits a greater freedom in terms of themes and styles pursued and working practises employed. Audiences can be challenged by exciting new work and avoid being patronised by the double-guessing of what 'they really want to see' which happens in so many mainstream theatres.

But equally the difficulties can be immense. Shortage of funding is an obvious one; trying to raise sufficient funding is time-consuming, complex and on-going. Gaining critical reviews is a major problem which is very difficult to overcome. As Sarah Kane mentioned, a bad review can kill a show dead. No review at all can mean little audience response and poor box office returns, which in effect can mean disaster for the company's future projects. Despite many claims by the likes of Michael Billington to support new writing and innovative theatre, reviewers still tend to frequent a selected range of Off-West End theatres and rarely venture out to the provinces. Pam Gems, whose work now largely consists of adaptation of novels for stage, appreciates the difficulties faced by the people passionate enough about their work, or desperate enough, to form their own companies:

> I really honour the people who have hung on.... They are the heroes and heroines. They don't make a buck, yet they go on doing play festivals and new writing. But it's hell. You're scraping by all the time, cap in hand. And we don't have enough patrons. But so often what you see on the Fringe has *life*. It might be formless, there might be a couple of bad performances, but it has life.[46]

Helen Edmundson now also spends most of her time adapting the works of others, writing original texts only about every five years. Whilst not denigrating the skills of the adapter, she likens adaptations to scoring penalties and original works to setting up and scoring an actual goal.

So are the alternatives as clear-cut as Mainstream, Adaptation, or Fringe? Probably not. But I feel the playwright/artist who chooses to work on the fringe would be foolish to expect mainstream recognition. Indeed some playwrights, such as Barker, feel that being labelled alternative, experimental or non-mainstream actually gives their work added credence. Bryony Lavery has come to terms with her limited recognition: "What does receiving mainstream recognition mean? That Billington likes you? Wow! Michael Coveney? I get very 'important' recognition from some very unimportant people!"[47]

Recognition seems to be the key word here - in the sense of recognition by others, who you want those 'others' to be, and how much you are prepared to adapt for their recognition. When you become involved in the theatre there needs to be a recognition of the world into which you are entering. Pam Gems compares the world of the theatre to that of the criminal:

> I remember talking to a criminal once and he said, 'The trouble is, you can't pick up a phone and take an order. You've got to get out there, fucking keep going after people and you never know where you are.' And I thought, 'Just like the theatre'. There's this kind of hierarchy, an inner circle, which really annoys me. It's horrible, but you have to wait to be picked, unless you get together and form your own power-base. Then you get respect. It may be grudging, but you get respect.[48]

This astute, if somewhat cautionary observation, is one which any playwright would do well to consider when writing for performance.

The playwright holds a unique position in the world of creative writers for whilst creating a literary text s/he has many audiences to consider apart from the initial reader. These audiences serve to influence and mediate the writer's work in many unseen and often insidious ways. The route from the page to the live performance space is often a difficult one, but one which I believe the playwright has to confront. For whilst the act of writing a play is immensely satisfying, taking that play into performance has to be the completion of that creative process.

Notes

1   L. Goodman, *The Routledge Reader in Gender and Performance* (London: Routledge, 1998), p. 111.

2   R. Williams, *Drama in Performance* (London: Penguin, 1972), p. 44.

3   S. Daniels, *Plays: 1* (London: Methuen, 1991), p. x.

4   *ibid.*

5   J. Derrida, *Writing & Difference* (London: Routledge & Kegan Paul, 1978), p. 134.

6   A. Wesker, 'Playing with the writer's rights' at Beyond Words Conference, Birmingham University, 1994.

7   E. Aston & G. Savona, *Theatre as Sign System* (London: Routledge, 1991), p. 142.

8   *ibid.*, p. 29.

9   R. Ingarden, *The Literary Work of Art*, 3rd edition (Northwestern University Press, 1973), p. 208.

10 quoted in H. Stephenson and N. Langridge, *Rage and Reason: Women Playwrights on Playwriting* (London: Methuen, 1997), p. 6.

11 *ibid.*, p. 11.

12 M. Bragg, *Rich* (London: Hodder & Stoughton, 1988).

13 quoted in Stephenson and Langridge, *op. cit.*, p. 23.

14 *ibid.*

15 *ibid.*, p. 37.

16 *ibid.*, p. 31.

17 *ibid.*, p. 102.

18 *ibid.*, p. 47.

19 J. Long, *What Share of the Cake Now?* (London: Theatre Studies and Cultural Studies at the University of North London, 1996), p. 40.

20 Keatley in Stephenson and Langridge, *op. cit.*, p. 74.

21 *ibid.*, p. xv.

22 *ibid.*

23 Long, *op. cit.*, p. 40.

24 quoted in Stephenson and Langridge, *op. cit.*, p. xii.

25 *ibid.*, p. xv.

26 quoted in M. Coveney, 'Backstage' in *The Observer*, 13 April 1997.

27 quoted in Stephenson & Langridge, *op. cit.*, p. xiii.

28 quoted in D. Glaister, 'ACE rhetoric, pity about the grants' in *The Guardian*, 16 February 1999.

29 P. Hall, 'He was our greatest hope now he leaves the country' in *The Guardian*, 27 March 1999.

30 quoted in Glaister, *op. cit.*

31 quoted in S. Tait, 'Is this a profit I see before me?' in *Weekend Financial Times*, Issue 30, November 1998.

32 *ibid.*

33 *ibid.*

34 *ibid.*

35 quoted in Stephenson and Langridge, *op. cit.*, p. 93.

36 *ibid.*, p. 73.

37 S. Daniels, *Plays: 2* (London: Methuen, 1994), p. xii.

38 quoted in Stephenson and Langridge, *op. cit.*, p. 134.

39 *ibid.*, p. xvi.

40 P. Nagy, *Plays: 1* (London: Methuen, 1998), p. xiii.

41 quoted in Stephenson & Langridge, *op. cit.*, p. xvii.

42 *ibid.*, p. 28.

43 K. Ireland, 'Programme notes' for *Und* (London: The Wrestling School, June 1999).

44 S. Berkoff, *Meditations on Metamorphosis* (London: Faber & Faber, 1995), p. xv.

45 quoted in Stephenson and Langridge, *op. cit.*, p. 18.

46 *ibid.*, p. 96.

47 *ibid.*, p. 106.

48 *ibid.*, p. 97.

2 Poetry and Performance

Tony Lopez

Performance's only life is in the present. Performance cannot be saved, recorded, documented, or otherwise participate in the circulation of representations of representations: once it does so, it becomes something other than performance. To the degree that performance attempts to enter the economy of reproduction it betrays and lessens the promise of its own ontology. Performance's being, like the ontology of subjectivity, becomes itself through disappearance. (Peggy Phelan[1])

May words cease to be arms; means of action, means of salvation. Let us count, rather, on disarray.

When to write, or not to write makes no difference, then writing changes - whether it happens or not; it is the writing of the disaster. (Maurice Blanchot) [2]

I have been thinking about the processes of writing and of performance which have been equally important for me at different times but mostly kept separate this far. This speculation comes at the point of a breakthrough in that divided practice because I recognize certain common elements in these processes that I wish to take further in giant steps. But first I need to move slowly in exposition, making clear some basic discriminations about poetry and performance in recent British and North American scenes. In doing so, I want to describe some ways in which writing and performance have a real and permanent connection which is more than what happens at any poetry reading, good or bad as that might be. I want to focus on the works of some performance writers of note and to relate what I see in their work to my own aspiration for a practice that fuses these interests, obsessions and desires.

We have in recent times had a series of "returns to the oral" in English language poetry which have sometimes provided interesting developments and destabilizing complexities for our conception of poetry but sometimes also led to no more than an oversupply of bardic wind. Deriving from the energies of the Beats, and especially from the large-scale success of Allen Ginsberg's public poetry in which he adopted the role of political activist and generational spokesperson, there was a 1960s revival of poetry readings that re-shaped the poetry of that time. British "protest poet" Adrian Mitchell and "jazz poet" Christopher Logue are credited with the beginnings of "non-specialist poetry readings" and soon after there was an explosion of interest with new kinds of poetry developing for the new hip youth audience.[3] In this climate the careers of poets such as Roger McGough, Libby Houston, Jeff Nuttall, Frances Horovitz, Michael Horovitz, Lee Harwood, Spike Hawkins and Brian Patten were established. At the time it must have seemed like a new movement of popular and populist poetry, but now it looks like the chaotic opportunist beginnings of various very different poetries some of which have not even survived.

More recently there have been punk and dub poets, performance poets, stand-up poets and poetry slams with their various champions. John Cooper Clarke, Joolz, Attila the Stockbroker, Linton Kwesi Johnson, Jean Binta Breeze, Benjamin Zephania, John Hegley and Murray Lachlan Young, all of them with an audience and all of them a necessary corrective to the tendency of academic remoteness that is perceived by each new potential audience coming across the difficulties or restricted vision of mainstream poetic culture. At its worse, however, this strand of "performance poetry" becomes rather less interesting than the pop music that it wishes to impersonate, which is at least the genuine expression and self-definition of youth culture through a connected sense of style in image, fashion and music. The end of this avenue is the marketing of the so-called "New Generation" poets as the new rock-and-roll, with their readings which are just book-promotion opportunities for Bloodaxe and Faber, as somehow connected to live performance.

Yet there is a poetry performance practice that is not reducible in this way to empty gestures of pop-imitation, stand-up or advertising. Particularly impressive in the British context is the work of Cris Cheek which builds on the performance element of avant-garde practice in the sound poetry of such poets as Bob Cobbing, Tom Leonard, Peter Finch, Edwin Morgan, Dom Sylvester Houédard but also on the work of Americans such as David Antin, Jackson Mac Low and Steve Benson. I have seen Cris Cheek making performances which are radical on-the-spot revisions of given texts and splicings of several texts, voice enhanced or interrupted by various musical and non-musical noises and special effects that make the event a deliberately non-repeatable performance of considerable power. I have found his performances of a post-colonial work *Skin upon Skin*, based in part upon Defoe's *Robinson Crusoe*, especially convincing for these technical reasons but also because the work itself is so ambitious in the way it stages the racism of the West in a non-academic "reading" of a classic text.[4]

The most self-aware practice in American poetry performance is the "talk poetry" of David Antin which is by no means a return to a simple or vatic oral poetics. Antin performs a talk poem by improvising a one-off speech in front of an audience, focusing on particular issues and philosophical questions and also telling stories about his relatives and friends. Stephen Fredman writes that Antin "by his invention of the talk poem challenges us to conceive of poetry, criticism and philosophy as a single activity".[5]

Antin tells us that his improvised performance of the poem is the only valid form of the work and that the printed form (a transcription of a tape recording) is a much lesser thing. 'Real Estate' (which I have only read printed in an anthology and not experienced as a performance) for all its rough and ready surface, seems to be carefully structured throughout its 26 printed pages. The status of the event in real time is stressed and a connection is made to Homer's *Odyssey* and *Iliad* – which he cites, plausibly enough, as being structured in their time by the occasion of performance. Antin continues with his thoughts about accents and different habits of speaking in different places, to develop a connection between language as cultural identity and

but i was beginning to realise that   as with a car   there
is a limit   on how long it can do it
                    and so i had the feeling that
in these pieces where i go out and talk its true that i regard
the pieces as the center   yet i still feel   thats because its
running out and i dont have time to go all over   to do the
pieces all over the world im not omnipresent in all places
talking to all the people i feel might benefit from hearing me
     talk   or   that i might want to talk to   because i enjoy the
idea of talking to people   i suppose i thought ill put these
things in books
           books are not ideal   i dont believe that books
are ideal forms   that is books are   imperfect recordings
    of transactions that occur in real time   im here now and im
trying to make a piece   the way artists   have probably
always tried to make real work once   and   at some point
ill take an imperfect record of what ive done   and   it will
    be an imperfect record because it will only be a tape recording
     and it will only get some of the effect of being here   because
what i say   to some degree   is determined by what you
     think   and my sense of it   otherwise id have to do an
     entirely separate   berkeleyian ego trip   where i would
talk about anything   independently of who i think you are
                  this is not my
approach to poetry   i suspect that   the approach to poetry
    of poets   in their natural   habitat   which is in
performance   and in performance improvisation   has
    always been   a response to some specific set of urgencies
      that is   homer told the story that way that time
(Antin, from 'Real Estate', in Messerli, p. 891)[6]

"Real Estate" (excerpt) by David Antin, from TUNING. Copyright © 1984 David Antin.
(reprinted by permission of New Directions Publishing Corp.)

language as currency (promise and declaration of value). This idea leads him back to his own simpler childhood sense of the value of money and from there he tells the story of his relatives who were refugees from Russia, one an artist who went to the USA and the other, Philip, a printer who went to work in a cigar factory in Argentina. Their survival and progress in American society was based first in their ability to become speakers of languages: Yiddish, Ukrainian Russian, Spanish and English. The two brothers are eventually united in New York and the wealthy brother's money is invested in land which later is developed as holiday-home for city dwellers, attracting a particular class of immigrant worker who wished to keep a connection to European culture. So the holiday development becomes a working-class intellectual summer camp, a sort of temporary republic of the mind. Then later the fortunes of the business change and the development becomes a liability.

The poem seems to be structured as a whole because the story of political activists escaping from Russia after the first unsuccessful revolution, then travelling through Latvia to Argentina and the USA, taking on different kinds of work, learning languages and managing to haul themselves out of poverty to become landowners and capitalists in their way has echoes of the world of Homeric epic. In Homer's story the hero and his companions voyaged round the known world dealing with new and alien challenges in each place. In Antin's talk poem the shift in values from revolutionary politics to land owning and development: the trust in land rather than money or other forms of investment, and then the loss of value in the development as the society alters around them, all these are well-told elements of the poem that follow with casual and deceptive ease. Money itself changes in value, and it becomes useless (later in time, earlier in the narration of the poem) when Antin tells how he was refused a hire car because he had plenty of cash but no credit card. The humorous connections between remote threads of these stories are instances of great facility in Antin's technique. The instability of values located anywhere other than in the human community is demonstrated throughout.

Yet there are claims made about Antin's performance that are impossible to substantiate from the text we have before us. He claims to be taking the audience into account

> otherwise id have to do an
> entirely separate berkeleyian ego trip   where I would
> talk about anything   independently of who i think you are

but we don't learn from the printed version anything about that audience whatsoever. Antin, according to the transcript, never stops talking, so his sense of the audience and its needs is not challenged. We can't tell from the transcript how he knows what their interests are, except we know that he must have some friends and admirers of his work there, since he was invited as a guest speaker. This idea of the audience is a phantom, therefore, in the mind of the performer. He may have opinions about what his friends know and like and wish to see, but the performance is not really responsive in any way except (possibly) that basic process of noticing when people have had enough of a particular thing. Even that is completely unreliable unless there is some real process of feedback incorporated into the event: for how can we know if one uncomfortable or tired person represents in herself a general feeling unless we stop and ask? The performance transcript is interesting, indeed profoundly moving to read and so this issue of being responsive has seemed less pressing than it might otherwise be. The performance is interesting also because it is live and because whatever memorized prompts and fall-back routines have been built into it, there is a projection of risk in the present that relates to the materials he brings to share.

A talking performance practice that makes radical moves from Antin's position is that of Steve Benson: the improvisation is looser, edging into danger, you don't know

what will happen next. I saw Benson's first UK performance at the Cambridge
Conference of Contemporary Poetry (CCCP) in March 1995 and it remains very clear in
my memory. He appears on the stage of the Keynes room in King's college, a strange
space, a lot wider than it is deep with a raised stage and a balcony over the stalls.
There is a bust of J.M. Keynes over to the right when you are facing the stage and Peter
Riley's bookstall is arranged nearby, a rare copy of J.H. Prynne's *The White Stones* stuck
up in a prominent position.[7] Steve Benson is standing waiting for the session to begin
and he's wearing a walkman with large earphones down around his neck. He is
introduced by Rod Mengham who says something about recent American poetry and
Benson's place in it as a practitioner of improvised and spontaneous work. Most
people in the audience don't know Benson's work except by reputation: some will
have read Geoff Ward's pamphlet on the Language poets, where Benson's work is
given some space.[8] Some have more direct knowledge, those involved with the journal
L=A=N=G=U=A=G=E.[9] The audience is good, the hall feels full up, there is a lot of
goodwill for overseas visitors who have been invited to perform.

Benson is slight and looks jumpy. He puts earphones on and listens to a tape that's
playing on the walkman. It must be at full volume because when he pulls the
earphones down again we can hear (the audience can hear) that there is something
playing on the tape. During the introduction to the performance we can hear
intermittent distorted voices coming through the walkman headset and his
introduction explains that he has specially pre-recorded this material from various
audio-books that he listens to when driving to and from his work as a therapist in a
day-treatment centre for emotionally disturbed children in New York state. So the tape
that we can't hear properly is made by arbitrarily splicing together literary works in
non-textual form and snatches of those voices are coming right through the
introduction, making a new collage. During the performance Benson talks, improvising
as he goes, sometimes speaking with the walkman headphones on and sometimes with
them off. We don't know whether he is repeating the material on the tapes or working
by free association with what he hears, or whether he is inventing his speech by
working against what has been previously dubbed. Some time into the performance,
helpers who seem to have been previously recruited approach the stage and hand
Benson small pieces of paper on which brief texts have been written. He uses these
interruptions as further prompts and deflections in the production of the performance.
In a sense I was included in this process as I had turned up with a tape recorder to
record the performance. Benson said that he needed a recording of the event and so I
agreed to send him a copy. This is an excerpt from his transcript of my tape-recording
of that performance:

> My grandma was very brown and old but her coarse shoes burnt in
> preparation for growling in a speech of desperation. He couldn't
> mend his bleary eyes, they were wide and crossed. His own voice
> was swiftly gathering at the department store and riding with the
> stairs as the escalator went up, it seemed to reach a kind of
> diabolical cancer, a sheer swollen mass of guilt and shame that

had been transformed in the most magical way into sparking objects and items. When you tore the packaging off, you found yourself running through so many layers that your hands became tired, and you couldn't think of anything more to see. It was miles from where we lived to where they had seen us there and after several minutes our voices subdued our own awe and called to say we are calmly thanking what washes in our come, the wheels revolving our asses and the mob looking.

I don't know what I mean, but that's not what I - that's not that horrible thought. It's simple and faithful, and it becomes more and more confident and tricky, because people need to rest between these onslaughts of imaginary coercion that are being projected out through our feelings into the purity of all this grasping greed and frustrated energy of - like I say, reaching for the separation of vision, which itself is likely to be not caused by but impregnated by a kind of carcinogenic influence from the sun, if you understand what I mean. It's a good quality in print, but in knowing it becomes critical. It reaches a critical mass, in fact, and we can't talk we just do, as in athletics. We are sure that we do right, but you return into the world honestly, coming to destroy her, as in the film last night, which was built like a penetrating ray or ribbon through my life. In it, it spoke to me further of my own death, and yours.

This was far away and the other time, exactly on the other side of time.

(from "The Beckoning, Reckoning Naught", Benson's
transcript of his 1995 Cambridge performance)[10]

Rough-jointed and discontinuous as it, the text seems to connect material from traditional fairy tales "grandma … growling … bleary eyes … transformation … horrible thought … diabolical … magical … to destroy her" and other matter such as (Christmas?) visits to department stores and the unwrapping of presents also relevant to childhood, with another thread running through the text of something like radiation anxiety: "desperation … cancer … imaginary coercion … carcinogenic influence … critical mass … penetrating ray … my own death and yours". Of course the conjunction of different materials is a common feature of postmodern writing, and would not be of special interest here except that the feedback of anxiety is so powerfully focused. If the fairy tale is a traditional means of coping with insurmountable challenges: bereavement, suicide, desertion, the powerlessness of children, fostering or adoption; or difficult social transitions such as entry into adulthood and sexuality, then the location of this generalised contemporary anxiety connecting to such a genre-framework redoubles the surplus of panic-ridden affect.

Benson's performance was clearly organized in a way to create the maximum emotional engagement between the invited performer and the audience. The fact that the speech was improvised from particular sources in a process that was visible before an assembled poetry audience (allowing for no rehearsal and no fall-back) means that the audience were bound to be either concerned for the performer: hoping that the performance would come off and provide an experience that was worthwhile; or else be involved in an equally concerned suspense: hoping for an amusing failure to develop. Both of these must be happening at once. In a sense this emotional investment is self-fulfilling, since one significance of the performance is the temporary construction of this fleeting sense of emotional involvement and particular shared experience. The performer's vulnerability becomes the meaning of the performance because it makes a connection between everyone in the room.

Of course this is the opposite of a poetry reading. There is no finished and published text, product of a careful and private process of crafting, that is read out to the audience. The sense of authority that comes from a definitive performance (the author must know how to do it) of a definitive printed text that the poet has and the audience often does not have, is completely undermined. The performance, rather than being a formal interpretation of a given text (in some sense a dramatic event), becomes instead a moment of composition, when the relatively raw first-draft material is generated. There would be little point in making a further performance with the same text, since almost all of the performance dynamic would be lost. Benson's published work, much of it collected in *Blue Book*, consists largely of edited transcriptions of performance events.[11] The writing is therefore made by the processes of performance and transcription and must, whatever else it is, be a form of art-documentation. This mixed status is significant, it seems to me, in the meaning of the work. Whichever arena it is judged in, it escapes neat categories and resists easy consumption, and the institutional acceptance of some Language writing doesn't alter this.

"Dint" was a commissioned work that I developed for "A Place that is Not A Place: A Seminar on Liminality and Text" at the Universidad Autonoma de Madrid in March 1997. This two-day seminar was organised by the Liminality Research Group at UAM who invited researchers from various different fields of literary studies to investigate the function of the concept of liminality in their particular fields. My paper "Innovation in Contemporary Poetry" was scheduled first and I was booked to give a performance to end the seminar. Throughout the conference I took notes by recording two-stress phrases, significant, blank, amusing or not, as individual lines in a notebook, listing them two columns to a page. I made no special effort to grasp or encompass the arguments of the papers in my notes but worked quite passively collecting material as the conference went on. In a sense the very passivity of this process was useful as I was free to actively listen to the papers at the same time, though I'm sure that my listening was subject to the same lapses as anyone else. As it progressed the event itself seemed to take on the characteristics of liminality that Victor Turner describes in *The Anthropology of Performance*.[12] A cut off feeling that is common in campus-based conferences was enhanced by each paper that developed the idea of a threshold to a special transitional or marginal state, whether of displaced persons and refugees, or actors or characters in gothic fiction. At the point of making the notes, I had made no decision about exactly how to use them and was expecting to take them back to England to work on much later.

Naturally the order of the notes follows the schedule of the seminar. For the performance at the end of the seminar I had planned to read some poems from *Stress Management* and to use slides I had with me to project one sequence from *False Memory* so that I could read it off the screen from among the audience.[13] *False Memory*, a work which is made of different specialist languages (medical, legal, political, advertising, business etc) spliced together into a synthetic continuity seemed ideal for the seminar. But at the beginning of the last session I realised that I could select from and re-arrange the material that I had written down through the seminar and make a new piece ready for performance at the end.

I therefore made a new version by choosing lines from the notes I had made, intuitively assembling lines that followed on or altered the potential meaning of each previous line, whilst turning back and forth through the notebook on which four columns were displayed on each double-page spread. The order of the lines in the notes was therefore completely altered but the process and rules of assembling were not consciously worked out in advance. The writing-editing process includes reading runs of lines together to see if they "go". For me the process of writing poetry always includes reading the work aloud and checking whether it works when spoken.

Of course the audience loved this piece because it gave them back fragments of their own papers which had been processed and transformed into a new work. In this way a connection to the audience was established, similar to the phenomenon I have described occurring in Benson's performance. The poem was produced out of the matter of the conference and also because of the pressure of a running schedule with a performance booked for a particular place and time. The papers that I used as source material were themselves based on the analysis of works by (for instance) Lorca, Ian Hamilton Finlay, Georges Perec, Washington Irvine, and Barrett Watten, so that there is an indirect connection between these works and "Dint", through the medium of my colleagues' readings of those texts. Though the subject-texts of the papers remain subliminal for a reader of "Dint", the papers that were my source material take on a liminal status by referring backwards to the source texts and by being altered into the matter of "Dint" which, in using them, partly detaches them from the previous connection.

Dint

no such antagonism	between these barriers
serves to restore	for verification
a vested interest	and this mode of bathos
in these fringe areas	in historical time
a conventional surface	slides into invention
trying to expel	a door to door salesman
the tighter sense	refuses to relinquish

scientific knowledge
crossing the threshold
a recent *X-files*
the remainder of this paper
most ingenious theories
along the Hudson river
it is however
a surplus of frames
according to the rules
waiting for the bus
or incompleteness
we are our memories
I'll just skip a bit
contact zones
barely perceptible
traces of wit
and hostile attributes
at first appear
seeking to outrun
the turn of the century
more detailed accounts
of the agent's movements
between these figures
wishing to combine
a genial character
replaced an object
on flagging lettuces
in no way sincere
natural or man made
textual communications
to capture a person
in the absence of history
various rectangles
seem more equivocal
but a poetry groupie
can function on all
inherently different
this kind of emphasis
two equally provisional
ontological dangers
of internal repetition
altered by fractals
a throwaway soldier
arrives at the airport

since it concerns
a criss cross web
emphatically denied
an ordinary citizen
in the war of ideas
a crucial distinction
refuses to send
where ethical systems
a victim of gothic
jumps through the mirror
in order not to
on a tiny island
is able to combine
a split allegiance
probably the wall
legalistic and geographical
a flat repetition
more like a dream
to avenge my family
fractures and divides
a genre of dance music
never ceases to imply
rational sequences
crossing out the word
an analogous function
in misrecognition
I'll take a drink
pursued by ghosts
declining into factions
which the natives consider
a regional conflict
prohibido fumar
she imagined a sister
in 1943
I still can't see
their indelible mark
for different reasons
merely the translator
a stranger in England
the pseudo memory
parodies authority
where the masquerade
enhances this danger
implicitly recognising

the excluded middle
and so invites
a life of tension
didn't find favour
you are not supposed
in the summer afternoon
a voice that is absent
looking for an exit
you take off your watch
sufficient to fracture
the cold war era
seems to contain
a series of steps
made of dead limbs
ever was contented
to fill its capacity
and be shadowed by
madness and obscenity
poses like a father
to report the crime

Performativity judged by reading the work aloud is for me the most important structuring device in composition. A collage of existing materials gets copied and re-copied, and reading aloud is the check for emotional, grammatical and rhythmical continuity. I'll put a new poem through this stage many times before I even begin typing it into the computer, and it is during the process of reading a new work aloud that much of it is invented, because words are produced out of the needs of specific instances of projected meaning and cadence. Then the typing and checking process adds further modifications which come from once again reading the printed script aloud. Each of these changes are checked by reading at first a passage and then the whole work to make sure that it is at all points consistent with my sense of its purposes when altered. But in the case of "Dint" where the work was more completely a collage than usual (there were only a very small number of invented lines), almost no words were added in the process. Rather the order of lines was altered until it seemed to work and substitutions were made, usually by altering the first word of a line to adjust the grammatical relations between lines.

But this description of working processes and structuring devices renders only a fraction of what it means to inevitably connect writing and performance in a meaningful way. The most significant aspect is the surrender of complete control in making something new. In performance one must surrender control because what happens, happens in real time, with all the unexpected contingencies that could meet a site-specific improvisation for a particular audience.

To prepare for an event through research or through training and rehearsal is not the same as an open-ended process of private revision. To accept a limit in these processes is liberating. To renounce control is not to renounce responsibility for what happens and what is produced. I realised some time ago that certain performances I made in the 1980s were a way of not writing because writing became for two or three years completely unbearable. I can only explain this silence as an appropriate response to a bad event which happened to me and my family, an event that I now understand as a delayed aftershock of World War II. Well what isn't? At this time, in May 1983, I met Joseph Beuys in Cambridge as he was preparing for a performance in the university and an exhibition of drawings in Kettle's Yard gallery.[14] It had been arranged with Anthony D'Offay, who organised Beuys' British exhibitions and appearances, that I would make a video recording of his performance and I went to meet him beforehand to discuss the project.

It was Beuys who in 1964 wrote to the authorities in East and West Berlin to propose that the Berlin wall be raised by five centimetres for aesthetic reasons. Later in 1964 he ran an action including a poster campaign whose message was "The Silence of Marcel Duchamp is overestimated". In 1974 he was wrapped in felt and caged for three days in a New York gallery with a coyote, a walking stick, and fifty copies of the Wall Street Journal. This performance, to which he arrived and left by ambulance, was called "I like America and America likes Me".[15] It was because of these art "actions" that I wanted to be involved in his Cambridge appearance. I was also at this point preparing a performance that would take place in less than a month, and the example of his work was thankfully just too blatant to ignore. Out of any matter by any means his art was made and all of it has a political and ethical dimension that cannot be escaped. I have only recently seen the collection of Duchamp work in Philadelphia, and now that slogan seems to alter in meaning each time I look at it. All of Beuys' art seems to be a response to events in World War II that we are only just now beginning to work out. So many people's lives seem to have been fundamentally fractured by the war, and not just those who, like Beuys, actively took part. I am still working through this sense of fracture and displacement.

In responding to Antin's talk poem "Real Estate" and to Benson's performance that I have described above, I am intending to situate my practice as much with those Americans as with Denise Riley, Tom Raworth, Allen Fisher or J.H. Prynne, whom I consider to be the most significant poets writing in Britain today.[16] But it is in a European context that these aesthetic considerations need to be set moving, since there is so much damage and potential damage that demands our urgent attention.

Notes

1   Peggy Phelan, *Unmarked: The Politics of Performance* (London: Routledge, 1993).

2   Maurice Blanchot, *The Writing of the Disaster*, translated by Ann Smock (Lincoln, Nebraska: University of Nebraska Press, 1995).

3   See Edward Lucie-Smith (ed), *British Poetry Since 1945* (Harmondsworth: Penguin, 1970) pp. 27-32 and 302; Pete Roche (ed), *Love, Love, Love: The New Love Poetry* (London: Corgi, 1967), pp. xiii-xiv.

4   Cris Cheek, *Skin upon Skin* CD (Lowestoft: Sound and Language, 1996).

5 Stephen Fredman, *Poet's Prose: The Crisis in American Verse* (Cambridge: Cambridge University Press, 1983), p. 135.

6 Douglas Messerli (ed), *The Other Side of the Century: A New American Poetry 1960-1990* (Los Angeles: Sun and Moon, 1994).

7 J.H. Prynne, *The White Stones* (Lincoln: Grosseteste, 1969); Prynne's poetry is most recently collected in J.H. Prynne, *Poems* (Newcastle upon Tyne: Bloodaxe, 1999).

8 Geoff Ward, *Language Poetry and the American Avante-garde* (Keele: British Association for American Studies, 1993), pp. 9-12.

9 See Bruce Andrews and Charles Bernstein (eds), *The L=A=N=G=U=A=G=E book* (Carbondale, Illinois: Southern Illinois University Press, 1984), which collects essays from the journal *L=A=N=G=U=A=G=E* volumes 1-3.

10 The full text of Steve Benson's 1995 Cambridge performance is published as "The Beckoning, Reckoning Naught", *Tongue to Boot* 2 (1995), pp. 52-58.

11 Steve Benson, *Blue Book* (Great Barrington, Massachusetts and New York: The Figures / Roof Books, 1988).

12 See Victor Turner, *The Anthropology of Performance* (New York: Performing Arts Journal Publications, 1986), p. 237; also *Dramas, Fields, and Metaphors: Symbolic Action in Human Society* (Ithica, New York: Cornell University Press, 1974), pp. 25-26.

13 Tony Lopez, *Stress Management* (London: Boldface press, 1994); *False Memory* (Great Barrington, Massachusetts: The Figures, 1996).

14 The touring exhibition *Joseph Beuys Drawings* was shown at the City Art Gallery, Leeds, Kettle's Yard Gallery, Cambridge and the Victoria and Albert Museum, London; there was an illustrated catalogue *Joseph Beuys Drawings* (London: Victoria and Albert Museum, 1983).

15 I read about these art events in Gotz Adriani, Winfried Konnertz and Karin Thomas, *Joseph Beuys: Life and Works*, translated by Patricia Lech (Woodbury, New York: Barron's Educational, 1979), and was therefore responding to imaginative reconstructions made out of photographs and eye-witness accounts; Beuys' performance work has since been very effectively documented in Uwe Schneede, *Joseph Beuys Die Aktionen* (Bonn: Gerd Hatse, 1994).

16 My paper 'Innovation in Contemporary Poetry', forthcoming from UAM is a reading of poems by Denise Riley, Allen Fisher, J.H. Prynne and Tom Raworth; the prosody of "Dint" owes much to Raworth's recent poems which may be found in Tom Raworth, *Clean & Well Lit: Selected Poems 1987-1995* (New York: Roof, 1996); recent anthologies of this poetry are Iain Sinclair (ed), *Conductors of Chaos* (London: Picador, 1996) and Richard Caddel and Peter Quartermain (eds), *Other: British and Irish Poetry since 1970* (Hanover, New Hampshire: Wesleyan University Press, 1999).

3 Minor Asides of Performance in Some Works of Iain Baxter and the N.E. Thing Company:
Beginnings to 1970

Lorenzo Buj

Back before I came to this great stage of fools, wawling and squalling in a damp Dalmatian winter, Iain Baxter would have learned the word 'ecology' as a zoology major at the University of Idaho, in Moscow, USA. Toads, frogs, bats, and birds were among the specimens on his table or in his eye as he prepared a B.Sc. in Biology between 1955 and 1959. He was headed, it seemed, for doctoral work in the life sciences, perhaps a career in forestry. But Madam Fortuna had already gazed down the vista of years and elected an alternate route. Studies under Earl Larrison, a University of Idaho zoologist, yielded work as a field researcher of rodent populations, co-authorship of an article on squirrel species in the potato state, and a position as illustrator for a guidebook, *Wildlife of the Northern Rocky Mountains*. You can still look it up as Volume 6 of the American Wildlife Region series, published in Healdsburg, California, by Naturegraph. The date on that is 1961, the same year in which the young animal illustrator receives a Foreign Scholarship from the Japanese government. He sets out with wife Elaine Ingrid for a nine-month stay at the University of Kyoto. The foreign sojourn will prove fruitful. Japan is salubrious and eye-opening. There son Tor (with the name taken from the term "satori") is born. There Baxter mounts a one-man show at the Yamada gallery of contemporary art. He presents his audience with abstract expressionist compositions painted over folding Japanese screens. The work is dynamic and fluent, but altogether formalist.

I recount these things as recalled by the protagonist himself, sitting across from me on two occasions: in the Faculty dining lounge in Vanier Hall at the University of Windsor, in the summer of 1994; and in the Director's chair of the University's School of Visual Art, in September 1996. Man is an animated ape when the music of chance plays propitiously upon his ears. Baxter's discourses put me in appreciation of correspondences and immigrant patterns. The Baxters returned from Japan by Christmas 1961, at just about the time that my own father interrupted his studies and university adventures in Zagreb, taking the seaward trip to Zadar for a first view of new mother and son. Seven years later my father would take his family to Canada, sailing into Halifax harbour aboard the *Cristoforo Colombo*, the very boat that Baxter and young Tor would board in 1971 for a return trip to the old world where Baxter was born in 1936 in Middlesbrough, UK. I have discontinuous, half-dreamt memories of

Venice, Piraeus, and Madagascar. Baxter tells me that our ship also docked in Boston and New York. Thus our intersecting lines of life and patterns of travel. The Mediterranean author and the North Atlantic artist.

Life's nonsense, I wonder, pierces us with a strange relation. Before our 1994 luncheon, I hastened to find a passage from Patrick Kavanagh, which had appeared as an epigraph in a book by Hugh Kenner that I had recently read. It would put perspective on Baxter's activities under the name of artist. I was thinking of Baxter treading the trail of Duchamp, one among others in the early Sixties. The epigraph was in Kenner's book on Irish modernism, which contends that the conquest of English by cunning and self-absorbed outsiders from the Emerald Isle has determined the course and contour of a good deal of Western literary culture in the twentieth-century. Kenner is the foremost North American critic on Ezra Pound, James Joyce, and the modernist era. He is also the bearer of a "pan-Celtic" pedigree, with "valued quarter[s]" of Welsh and Scottish blood added to "[a] portion" of English, and God knows what else.[1] From Kavanagh he quotes as follows: "[w]hat the alleged poetry-lover loved was the Irishness of a thing. Irishness is a form of anti-art. A way of posing as a poet without actually being one".[2]

The date on this citation is as fitting as the pun that might be manufactured out of its Irish guts. In 1963 daughter Erian is born, and Baxter is painting his way toward the end of a Master's Degree in Fine Arts at Washington State University in Pullman. He produces large, hard-edge abstractions with stylized organic motifs, such as were current in the works of Ellsworth Kelly and Jack Youngerman. As a graduate student working in the prevailing style, with colour and shape and canvas-edge as dominant aesthetic issues, Baxter hadn't emancipated himself from the formalist model set forth by Clement Greenberg. But he was already indisposed to believe in art as a discrete category ideally free of social entanglements, with formal problematics as an intrinsic concern. Within a year he would leave the USA to teach at the University of British Columbia (UBC), where he undertook experiments with performance and started producing plastic, vacuum-formed works from the shapes of ordinary objects. It is with this early interest in the replication and altering of everyday commercial objects that Baxter's essential outlook on life and the function of art had begun to emerge, and is best characterized by adapting Kavanagh: *What the alleged art-lover has always loved is the Anythingness of a thing. Anythingness is a form of...etc.*

Baxter's place in the story of Canadian art after Abstract Expressionism begins with puns of this very sort - the *Anythingness* of the art he made and discovered with the Company that he founded in 1966 and incorporated in January 1969 as the N.E. Thing Co. Ltd. (NETCO), with his wife as Vice-President. Indeed, it is the *Anythingness* of outlook that first turns Baxter away from abstract painting and toward his eventual act as Company man. From the outset, his Company simulated and satirized the corporate structuration of contemporary life and the global embrace of the information age. But it wasn't primarily a critical enterprise, an art-world platform for ideological polemics or economic protest. In the spirit of Parisian Dada, Iain and Ingrid were rather more appetitive, drawn to happenstance and random acts of perceptual creativity. Company communiqués describe an entrepreneurial operation devoted to the research, evaluation, and development of Sensitivity Information (SI) and the identification of Aesthetically Claimed or Rejected Things (the ACT and ART departments). The Company was intended to sensitize and make possible more relations between this and that. If, in passing, it presented a mimicry of big business, major art, and cultural centrality, these were measures meant to liberate aesthetic energies when the question of objecthood had dissolved or dispersed into altered forms.[3]

The N.E. Thing Company was a home-based enterprise working out of North Vancouver. The domestic headquarters was set against background scenes of natural plenty and within the social milieu of Canadian West Coast art in the Sixties. Vancouver was the terminal town of the trans-Canadian railway and a pathbreaking outrider on a number of cultural fronts, matching or outstripping the advances usually attributed to such established metropolitan centres as New York and Los Angeles at other points of the continental slab. Recent panegyrics portray the city as one of the important North American nodes for the genesis, reception, and relay of conceptual ideas.[4] Neodadaism was the prevailing aesthetic and Baxter was a conceptualist in the prankish line of Duchamp. He also had associations with Vancouver's Intermedia collective, which was founded in 1967 and flourished into the early Seventies. Cliques and cabals, and solitary explorers, were active everywhere. The Baxters imbibed the ambiance, but stuck to their own program. Iain was naturally friendly, open-minded and abounding in ideas, but also shrewd. "[H]e was not," as David Silcox has noted, "really a joiner or part of a specific faction, being somewhat too selfish, in a cheerful way, for that".[5] Behind the playful personality there was an earnest puissance of purpose. Baxter's "energy" and "ambitious drive" made him a "potent force," says Silcox. And Ingrid? She "encouraged, shared and contributed to the vitality that wrapped itself around everything that was done then".[6]

The N.E. Thing Company might never have evolved as it did without Baxter's passion for the thinking of Marshall McLuhan, who attained instant celebrity with the publication of *The Gutenberg Galaxy: The Making of Typographic Man* in 1962 and *Understanding Media: The Extensions of Man* in 1964. McLuhan rhapsodized about the exteriorization of the human nervous system in the age of global communications, inspiring the ecologically-minded Baxter with the notion that a new, symbiotic coexistence between human consciousness and technical apparatuses might yield a more holistic experience of reality. Baxter knew that technology was a prophylaxis against organic sensitivity, but with McLuhan he held the providential view that it was also a diversifier of connections, a cognitive prosthesis and a potential key to higher ecologies.

McLuhan delivered a set of influential lectures at UBC in February 1964, at an annual Festival of the Contemporary Arts. That summer, Baxter arrived to take up his teaching tenure at that institution, and by the following February he was one of the organizers and impresarios for an elaborate Festival event devoted to McLuhan's theories: *The Medium is the Message*, "the first epic, collaborative, outer-edge, cross-bred, audience-participation, multi-media piece of show biz invented by purely local [Vancouver] thinkers and doers".[7]

In the autumn of 1964 Baxter employed non-verbal teaching techniques during his first year on the job at UBC. He used mannequins, props, street signs, a tape recorder, and slides projected onto his body. He also appeared in bathing suit and flippers, 'swimming' on the classroom floor. In one of the photographs from these teaching sequences we see Baxter wrapped in plastic and performing the free-style crawl. As pedagogy, the action was mildly novel. As performance, it was somewhat slight, but it embodied the themes that would motivate his work in the next half-decade, the best five or six years of his career. The expenditure of energy even in the most graceless kind of swimming is more fluid than Baxter's flopping about on the ground in front of his students. But the performer's body is for Baxter always primarily a means, a generative device for expanded aesthetic sensitivity. The activity of swimming and the phenomenology of motion is abstracted, made to look awkward and futile, for the sake of a metaphorical visualization. The body isn't activated so as to dramatize personality or psychological depth. Rather, it is intended to catalyze fresh syntheses and undo purely analytic or purposive acts of perception. It is employed as a conductor of sensory data that the audience should freely convert to intellectual or emotive uses of its own. Materials and gestures are elements in this transmission process, as multivalent in their potential significance as the performer himself. Our understanding of water and other fluids, with their differing properties, is imaginatively enlarged by its metaphoric association with plastic, itself a material of varying densities.

In an interview from 1967 Baxter would spell out the core of his artistic vision:

> The world is made up of pieces of information of all kinds, visual or sensory. A fork, a car, a door; a handle or a rock - all these things are information; and if you can get beyond the label-attitude, you are able to see and experience all they contain. The label is what gets in the way of experience. Because an object is labelled a 'glass', people see simply g-l-a-s-s. They do not see all the intrinsic potential of 'glass-ness': how the glass is a bubble: how it's a container that captures space: how it's a clear window into some other little world. And then there's the whole other tactile experience, as well as the visual one, of drinking out of a variety of glasses: watching the fluid come up, sensing it flow into different shapes. People don't go off into these various realms of magic and empathy, pure form and surrealism, because labelling has become what their appreciation of life is. They have lost their innocent way of looking and feeling, and they start drilling it out of their kids at the age of six.
>
> All artists, all painters and sculptors are simply 'visual-sensory informers': people who handle our world's information, putting it together in colours and shapes.[8]

The child of six represents Baxter's deepest beliefs in aesthetic play and experimentation as a means of rejuvenating the senses and renewing the world. The concern for the child's obstructed growth is another way of asserting that the creative processing of "information" is the special talent of our species - a capacity that entails all possibilities of social and personal progress if only we could find ways to let it flourish. There is a transcendentalist dimension in such sentiments. Baxter's attitudes are prospective and global in scope. He hopes to create fresh constituencies outside of the art world, bridging the activities of the artist and the commercial imperatives at work in wider society.

Lest the idea of such tactical reconciliations should sound undigested, we might consider how Baxter, in "simply" taking up the occupation of a "visual-sensory informer", stood in relation to those other views of the artist still current in Europe at that time. Yves Klein comes to mind, issuing a special newspaper featuring a doctored photograph of his celebrated "Leap into the Void". With his levitational metaphysics, he was the Simon Magus of the art world, as Joseph Beuys was a shaman working with a repertoire of densely symbolic materials. Baxter, meanwhile, was a creative pragmatist in the line of Ralph Waldo Emerson and Henry David Thoreau, an author he much enjoys. He wanted to refresh our powers of perception and diversify our cognitive patterns by attending to the multiple associations embedded in ordinary things such as water and plastic, or experimenting with new technologies of the late Sixties such as telecopier and Telex. It is not the transformation of subjectivity – a deep concept – that was at the core of his work, but the construction of multiple contacts between two systems: the perceptual-conceptual complex of the mind and the indiscerned or hidden properties of everyday things, which may include natural elements as well as mass produced commodities.

In February 1966, some five months before the formation of the N.E. Thing Company, Baxter installed *Bagged Place*, a fully-furnished four-room apartment in the UBC Fine Arts Gallery. Everything from walls and lamps, to couches and chairs, toilet, feces, and toilet paper, foodstuffs and reading material, was sealed in plastic. The exhibition flyer included a rental notice, which also ran in the local papers:

> **Bagged Place** – 4 rm. self-contained furn. ste., double bed, plastic bagged, sterilized, scenic view, close to U.B.C., no students, non-smoker, non-drinker, no pets or children, parking in rear. Open for insp. daily except Sunday from Feb. 2.

As an interactive feature of this installation, the audience was invited to enter the apartment and Baxter himself could be seen using the space, laying back on a bagged bed, perusing the pages of a bagged book. The installation brought Baxter his first substantial amount of notoriety and would anticipate the later environments that he and his wife would construct, use, and occupy as Company Presidents. Significantly, Baxter's advertisement outlined a "plastic bagged, sterilized" space with a "scenic view". Such a mediated relationship to landscape and nature would later be the subject of the eight-piece series entitled "Suite of Canadian Landscapes" (1969) where Canadian banknotes ranging in value from $1 to $1,000 were matted, framed, and signed. The backs of the bills present delicate, engraved views of cross-country vistas, from rushing rivers to oceanic coasts, prairie flats to mighty mountains, farm settings and winter landscapes. In imposing a second order of aesthetic enframement (the scenes on the bills are already bordered and printed with the ciphers of specific value), Baxter was connecting the enjoyment of "scenic views" on walls or through windows to market forces and national ideals. He was bringing to light the continuum of hidden links between residential environments and household commodities, and the organic spaces of great, Canadian nature.

Linking the N.E. Thing Company's art to its operations base in suburban
Vancouver, Nancy Shaw observed how

> [t]he B[ritish] C[olumbia] government aggressively promoted its industrial resource base
> while presenting the province as an edenic, exotic and fantastically varied vacationland....
> Official promotion always obscured the fact that the so-called modernization of B.C.'s
> landscape through tourism and industrialization shaped frontiers for money making.[9]

Throughout the later Sixties, the N.E. Thing Company reacted with its own
manipulation of mass technologies and corporate forms, generating parodic and ironic
comments on commodity leisure in the great outdoors. It traversed, mapped, and
bagged Canadian geographies and institutional environments so as to demonstrate the
material and ideological challenges that aesthetic optimism would have to overcome in
achieving a qualitative transformation of life. Bagging household objects and whole
rooms compelled audiences to reflect on a process from its endpoint, alluding to the
conversion of natural resources into everyday products and disposable commodities,
fetishes with a short shelf life.

Baxter's fascination with plastic and packaging was but one aspect of a theatrical
aesthetic that connected his work to other art-world trends of the Sixties. Baxter's
eclecticism of means put him among the first postmodern, that is, post-painterly,
generation of artists. It is this generation that Michael Fried held responsible for
dismantling high-modernist sensibility and exploiting tendentious links between the
individual arts. Writing in *Artforum* in 1967, Fried concluded a long, complex article
entitled 'Art and Objecthood' with a series of censorious theses on recent
developments in sculpture. His judgements on this latest work were unambiguous:
"[w]hat lies between the arts is theatre," and "[a]rt degenerates as it approaches the
condition of theatre".[10] At one level, Fried's argument was over the evident impurity of
such works as a Rauschenberg bed-painting or Morris's prop-like columns, objects that
confused generic categories and generated their effects by declaring their material
status rather than striving to rise above it. By asserting the literalness of the materials
out of which they are made, these works fail to convey us beyond themselves.
Transcendence is what they reject. Rather than elevating sensibilities through richness
of association, they induce attitudes of *interest* and perplexed fascination.

In essence, Fried was concerned with the material basis of meaning in art. In multi-
media works that shattered generic distinctions between painting and performance,
sculpture and music, *meaning,* he felt, could no longer be qualitative, intrinsic in forms
or materials masterfully and conscientiously worked. Meaning was henceforth the
effect of theatre, that is, generated by contexts of relationality and broken boundaries
between the arts. Moreover, as distinctions dissolve or become adulterated, so do one's
convictions about the seriousness of an artist's relationship to tradition (as expressed
through his committed exploration of the essential forms and properties of the genre in
which he works) and the power of art to affect us at the most mysterious levels of
human sensibility. Using as an instance Anthony Caro's "best work" at the close of the
essay, Fried described the effects of falling under its spell, or, as he puts it, into its

"grip" where "one's view of the sculpture is, so to speak, *eclipsed* by the sculpture itself". In such a situation, the work manifests a "a continuous and entire presentness, amounting, as it were, to the perpetual creation of itself". The beholder experiences this as a moment of transcendental temporality, a heightened

> kind of *instantaneousness*: as though if only one were infinitely more acute, a single infinitely brief instant would be long enough to see everything, to experience the work in all its depth and fulness, to be forever convinced by it.

To this point, Fried's article had advanced a detailed and aversive reaction to the reduced art of Tony Smith, Morris, and Judd. It is clear from this passage, which resembles the situation in Rilke's poem "Archaic Torso of Apollo", why Fried should oppose the indeterminate qualities of works that are literal and objective, that present themselves as things whose mysteries do not verge on the next world and allow no fixed conviction as to the qualitative value of the experience that one is having. What Fried requires of art is the achievement of total presence, an effect arising out of "certain unknown and mysterious laws" that "move us in a particular way" and produce, in Clive Bell's memorable term, "significant form".[11] Behind such an aesthetic is a metaphysics of beauty and presence that should eclipse the redundancy and inconclusiveness of time. But the Minimalist art of Fried's day was devoted to just the opposite effect: "the literalist espousal of objecthood amounts to nothing other than a plea for a new genre of theatre; and theatre is now the negation of art". Fried detailed the confrontational aspects of such art, how it not only shared the viewer's space but stood in his way, "extort[ing]" a "special complicity". Morris's fibreglass L-beams and wedges, Judd's boxes and Andre's firebricks, these created situations that were "indeterminate, open-ended – and unexacting" as "the beholder [was] made aware of the endlessness and inexhaustibility if not of the object itself at any rate of his experience of it".

Baxter would have been the target of Fried's animus if only for the section of metal fence that he displayed in a gallery in 1967. It was a plain chain-link fence with a gate, which Baxter had first spotted as a consumer sample. A common object, a piece of prefabricated information appropriated and installed with no change to its form or structure. Outside of the gallery the fence functioned as both a barrier (use value) and a commodity (exchange value). Within the gallery it was employed as an occasion for public use, something to be seen and touched. Baxter intended that new patterns of information would emerge from the odd context of encounter. Since a length of fence installed in an empty gallery setting seems perfectly useless, the process of interaction should generate unexpected meanings and associations. The fence would be casually, playfully used to undo modes of existing awareness and to open up the field of mental functioning. In getting people to walk through it, lean over, push in the gate, Baxter was showing that the mind may be driven toward new frontiers through the most elementary activities. Climbing about an ordinary fence may not usually result in a flash of mental expansion, but for Baxter it was certain that such unscripted activities are always potential conditions for a breakthrough. For what is being released is a process through which the mind may surprise and surpass itself. Freedom is at work and what happens is that the mind, as Lyotard says, "should generate occurences before knowing the rules of this generativity".[12] Baxter's goal was the breaking of consensus patterns and the cleansing of sensibility, all carried forth under the rubric of a "research" situation. In 1968 Baxter issued a Company Statement that described the "N.E. Thing researchers ... probing ... the why and how of visual things and their combinations" in an "effort to discover distinct properties of effects and the means of putting them into operation". Although the rhetoric here was certainly satirical of the product-oriented nature of corporate thinking, the experimental intent was in earnest, and a mass-produced segment of fence was as good for Baxter's purposes in 1967 as a bottle-rack had been for Duchamp in 1913.

The "research" dimension of Baxter's art was sometimes presented as outright foolery, a preoccupation with whimsy or word play. But always it was intended to contravene unnecessary boundaries or habitual limits and to uncover new angles of perception. The twenty-eight Kodacolor prints showing Iain as "President of a Company Blowing Bubbles" (1969), like the accompanying series of sixteen prints showing Ingrid as "President of a Company Face Screwing" (1969), are an absurdist homage to Muybridge's stop-action photographs of human motion. Whereas Muybridge broke down basic actions (kicking a ball, climbing a ladder, etc.) into discrete sequences, the Baxters applied the scientific format of his studies to an exhibition of the idle and infantile amusements of two Company bosses. The works were also cut with a parody of Warhol's celebrity multiples and, of course, sexual punning: the man blowing out a steady stream of bubbles; the woman stretching mouth and tongue, and pulling the whole face into twisting figures.

What happens when you try this or that? The Baxter method. Playing with anything that comes his way or pops out of the uncoalesced, optative jumble of his creative head. The outcome of said play, invention, or assemblage is an anti-product which assures the viewer that he should piggy-back on the author's whimsy, appreciate his conceptual sophistication, and proceed toward an intuitive state of improved innocence.

Every time Baxter makes a barb or cops a laugh, every time his work occasions an involuntary eruption, a bodily response – call it a chuckle, an expulsion of happy air - he provokes a forward movement beyond the boundaries of the art world. The movement begins within the subsidized settings and bureaucratic mechanisms of that "world" and then strives outward, as it were, in the name of integrative connections, perhaps even redemptive relationships with whatever is there. Thus his contacts with ephemera, his palpable empathies with pretty *paysage*, his vested play with the products, signs, images of our consumer world is a pre-Oedipal romance with the world's body. He poses credulously as a parasitic infant, exploring, tweaking, laughing his way across the thousand plateaus of this age. Yet his open, seemingly boundless sensitivity to everything of all sorts has also been used to reflect a devolution in the utopian legacy of the *avant-garde*, whereby the distance between the two worlds of "art" and "life" should shrink, with the immanent expansion of the former and the amelioration of the latter. The N.E. Thing Company kept pace with the *zeitgeist*, foregrounding the economy rather than upholding the autonomy of art, and revealing the minimal powers of purchase that aesthetics, divorced from the mechanisms of the market or its promotional strategies, could have on modern life.

For one month in 1969, the N.E. Thing Company was invited to occupy the first floor of the National Gallery building in Ottawa and carry on with its full range of operations. The "N.E. Thing Co. Environment" was officially opened on June 3 by Ron Basford, Canadian Minister of Consumer and Corporate Affairs; and a conference on "Visual Sensitivity Information, Communications, and Ramifications" was held on 6 June. The Gallery's existing floorplan had been significantly modified with the erection of additional walls and newly created office spaces. Desks, telephones, and typewriters were moved in and a secretarial area was also established. Security guards were on the premises and the N.E. Thing Company President came daily to work, transacting business and receiving visitors. A large display space featured Company products, with regular noon-hour demonstrations held for tour groups. Among the featured items were inflatable sculptures, a Carrying Bag for a Cumulous Cloud, and wearables such as the Baxters had shown the previous autumn in Burnaby, B.C. at an "Artists in Fashion" exhibit. In the women's line, these wearables included bikinis in pink vinyl; large, billowy vinyl tunics that "reach into space and cause the wearer to become more aware of his body as an armature for sculptural possibilities"; and transparent vinyl dresses that could be filled with coloured liquids or alcoholic spirits.

In September 1969, Iain and Ingrid, along with the critic Lucy Lippard, made a long journey to Inuvik in Canada's Northwest Territories. Here, within the Arctic Circle, Lippard was photographed walking a quarter-mile through tundra, toward true North. In two other projects, Baxter himself stood looking toward true North for one minute, using a compass for precise orientation; and urinated onto snow and ice, producing, as it were, a "Territorial Claim" that had already been "performed at Cape Spear, most Easterly point in North America and inside the Acropolis at Athens".[13] Both N.E. Thing Company Presidents also completed a 3.5 mile walk around the perimeter of Inuvik, taking pictures of the process and measuring the 10,314 steps it took with a pedometer. The far North was significant for its degree of territorial remoteness from the art world and its centres. As recorded, the projects in and around Inuvik combined exploration and banality, simple scientific technique and irregular acts of mapping. The N.E. Thing Company was measuring space and time as a way of quantifying, abstractly and symbolically, the ephemeral nature of psychic information. The vast wilderness setting was an extreme planetary contrast to the simulated realities of installations in a high-traffic urban setting. In the solitary Arctic walks, as in the construction and use of corporate environments and bagged places, the self was put in a position to develop fresh patterns of psychic association and new forms of cognitive attunement.

Almost all the N.E. Thing Company projects were open-ended "research" events, roughly outlined, rather than expressions of artistic inwardness or schemes that should result in perfect closure. The goal wasn't the achievement of a substantive breakthrough, an attainment of conclusive fulness, emotional or intellectual. As President of the N.E. Thing Company, the artist was more pragmatic than metaphysical of temper. The world's abundance of data offers a multitude of contacts and passages, and the art becomes an exploration and a testing of brief forms and processes. As the

Iain Baxter in 'Bagged Place', February 1966. The public participated by walking through an apartment in which all contents were wrapped in plastic. It was installed for two weeks. There was real food in the kitchen area and on the dining table, plus an actual piece of defecation in the toilet – bagged, of course.

basic unit of reality is information in a fluid and instantaneous state, the performing body is almost purely a means, rather than self-consciously an object or subject. The body carries the psyche into fresh sensual configurations and is the organic means of its conceptual extensions. It is an operative site, an apperceptive nexus for the creation and study of psychic fluctuations.

Baxter's parodic role-playing as President of a corporation was often a reaction to the systems and structures of the art-world. And as that world was increasingly being affected by the emergence of electronic environments and media technologies, he decided he must also take his cause into contexts dominated exclusively by business prerogatives. In June 1970, the N.E. Thing Company was present at the Vancouver meeting of the Information Processing Society of Canada and the Canadian Operational Research Society; and later that month rented a space and set up a display at the International Data Processing Conference and Business Exposition in Seattle. Baxter played the role of an artistic interloper, attempting to vary corporate behaviour while toying and experimenting with transmission technologies. On both occasions he was employing forms of guerrilla theatre. In Vancouver he wore "somewhat baggy corduroy jacket and tartan tie ... look[ing] very different from the other grey-suited exhibitors". He and Ingrid posed with a large red Stop sign on which "GO" was printed and stocked their booth with exhibition catalogues and a television "featuring psychic mandalas vibrating to raga music".[14] To anyone who would listen Iain handed out buttons and spoke about "GNG - Gross National Good", opposing it to the byproducts of GNP, "things like pollution and urban sprawl". The same message was delivered in Seattle, where Baxter also distributed brochures that offered the N.E. Thing Company's consulting services and presented its view of a humanistic, culturally sensitive business community.

Since October 1969 Baxter had been sending out concrete poetry, graphic work, and photographs from a telex installed at N.E. Thing Company domestic headquarters in North Vancouver or the telecopier in the demonstration room of the Xerox office in the city core. These works explored the dialectic of imagination and information as mediated and conditioned by the latest commercial communication technologies. Some of these experiments with long-distance communication included Baxter sending instructions for activities and art shows to be mounted at remote sites. Essentially, he was fascinated by the powers of acting at a distance, of partially authoring events.

In the Spring of 1970 he sent a "Telexed Self Portrait From Memory" to Kynaston McShine, Associate Curator of Modern Art at MoMA, followed by later transmissions of full-length Polaroid photographs of himself, back view only. The telex piece was a verbal description of the five sides of Baxter's head, produced without the benefit of a mirror immediately at hand. The "Front Side" entry begins at the hairline and moves downward past the chin:

> Course [sic] brown hair slightly balding at temples and slightly over ears width of nose normal average lips side burns to bottom of ears fair complexion hazel eyes long eyelashes black non-protruding chin adams apple gold cap on front right tooth space between eyes short distance navy blue turtle neck sweater.

The passage is certainly a text and not a portrait, the visual line by line imitation of a sitter. An abstract linguistic code is transmitted in lieu of an ostensibly more concrete visual totality. Ever the critical trickster, Baxter was playing in the aporetic 'spaces' of representation, the gaps of equivalence or translatability between word and image, word and thought. Academic analyses of such discontinuities of sign and world were then just emerging as French structuralism and deconstruction were beginning to revolutionize the critical vocabulary of Anglo-American intellectuals. But Baxter was after an effect not quite bound within the nomenclature of semiotics or sign theory. Three informational processes spanning great space and discrete temporal segments were activated: Baxter's perceptual memory; linguistic description; and McShine's impossible reconstruction of the visual referent encoded by the telexed text. The two mental events, Baxter's mnemonic self-depiction and McShine's reconstruction of that first construction, were structured around the relative stability of a shared language, an informational system whose rules of operation are here violated by lack of punctuation, a spelling error, and syntactical ambiguity. The two mental events were in fact imaginary activities, temporary achievements of what Baxter would call fresh "psychic postures" created by media technology.[15]

Through deep and intuitive solidarity with McLuhan's thinking, Baxter was the first artist in Canada to anticipate the electronic era of art, when all is transacted or enunciated at the level of 'information'. In disposing himself toward McLuhan's vision of social reality as a scene of of intense data exchange, with psychic flow mediated by telephone, television, radio, and telex, Baxter discovered that the whole sphere of art and culture, and not just the boundaries between genres, were subject to the theatrical conditions created by new informational economies. It was an insight that guided further "research" into the Seventies and had a lasting influence on General Idea, the multi-media and performance collective that learned the most from the N.E. Thing Company's work in the previous decade.

Notes

1   *A Colder Eye: The Modern Irish Writers* (New York: Knopf, 1983), p. 12.

2   ibid, p.13.

3   A cogent discussion of these interrelated goals and activities, analyzed in terms of cultural centre and periphery, is presented in William Wood's 'Capital and Subsidiary: The N.E. Thing Co. and the Revision of Conceptual Art', in *You Are Now in the Middle of a N.E. Thing Co. Landscape*, pp. 11-23.

4   See Derek Knight, *N.E. Thing Co.: The Uniquitous Concept* (Oakville, On.: Oakville Galleries, 1995), p. 10, n. 17 and 18, and passim.

5   David Silcox, 'Remembering the N.E. Thing Company', in *You Are Now in the Middle of a N.E. Thing Co. Landscape*, p. 61.

6   *ibid.*, p. 61.

7   Alvin Balkind, quoted in Marie Fleming, *Baxter* [2]: *Any Choice Works 1965-70* (Toronto: Art Gallery of Ontario, 1982), p. 93, Note 15. The title of Balkind's essay is 'Body Snatching: Performance Art in Vancouver; a View of its History'.

8   See the 1967 section of the *N.E. Thing Co. Ltd. Book, Volume I* (no place of publication listed; unpaginated; 1978). Within its pages the publication is described as a 'Compendium of Company Ideas, Activities & Works' issued in connection with a 1978 show at Kunsthalle Basel.

9   'Siting the Banal: The Expanded Landscapes of the N.E. Thing Co.', in *You Are Now in the Middle of a N.E. Thing Co. Landscape*, p. 30.

10 See 'Art and Objecthood', reprinted in *Minimal Art: A Critical Anthology*, ed. Gregory Battcock (New York: Dutton, 1968), pp. 116-47, for these and all subsequent quotations.

11 'The Aesthetic Hypothesis', in *Modern Art and Modernism: A Critical Anthology*, ed. Francis Frascina and Charles Harrison (London: Harper & Row, 1982), p. 69.

12 Jean-Francois Lyotard, *The Inhuman: Reflections on Time*, trans. Geoffrey Bennington and Rachel Bowlby (Stanford: Stanford UP, 1991), p. 72.

13 See the 1969 section of the *N.E. Thing Co. Ltd. Book, Volume I*.

14 See the 1970 section of the *N.E. Thing Co. Ltd. Book, Volume I*.

15 Quoted in Marie Fleming, *Baxter* [2]: *Any Choice Works 1965-70*, p. 90.

4 Collaborative Practice and the Phenomenal Dancer
Yolande Snaith's Theatredance

Ruth Way

There is currently a renewed commitment to develop an understanding of the creative processes in which choreographers/artists engage to facilitate their choreographic work. This chapter seeks to reveal the interconnectedness of creative processes and the evolution of choreographed performance. Choreographers, skilled artists who craft bodies in space, are constantly applying, inventing, re-inventing, and re-shaping creative processes which serve as catalysts for, and also function as tools to assist in, the formation of their work.

Through discussion with artists themselves we can begin to form an authentic picture of the methodologies and artistic sensibilities which nurture and inspire these creative processes and choreographic practice. For this purpose, I interviewed British choreographer Yolande Snaith, attempting to reveal her practice through an analytical, theoretical and philosophical enquiry into her most recent performance work.

Locating Theatredance

Snaith applies the term "theatredance" to her work and this label purposefully sets its dance elements in a theatrical context, drawing upon the significance of their performative relationship. She is defining her own work in a way which embraces the fusion of movement, music and/or sound, speech, characterization, and scenography present in the performance nexus to create intention and meaning, as well as seeking out the potential in each of these components which is then embedded in the choreography.

Since the 1980s, the term 'physical theatre' has been used to describe work of a hybrid nature where dance, text, design and sound collaborate to support choreographic intention. In her article, 'Charting the Road Towards a Physical Theatre', Ana Sanchez-Colberg proposes that

> the genre is not only a set of stylistic features of a production which is bodily based but rather one which extends discursive practices within the relative and tense relationship between the body-text-theatre reality which goes beyond mere representation via the body.[1]

It is possible to apply this framework to Snaith's work as well, and consider her "theatredance" as an embodiment of the dynamics between performer, narrative, space, and the very act of performing. She manipulates objects, furniture and costume to create allegorical representations; she explores their physical properties and their very positioning in the space. The presence and placement of these elements become embedded in the stage imagery and act in themselves as powerful agents in the creative process.

The precise meaning of terms such as "dance theatre", "theatre dance" (as others present it), and "physical theatre" is currently the subject of vigourous discussion and debate, especially in light of recent choreographic developments which have reinstated the importance of narrative content and meaning. Attempting to define "dance theatre", Rachel Duerdon and Neil Fisher write:

> as soon as other component parts take on greater importance in a dance performance, the shifting parameters give rise to questions surrounding the nature of dance and its relation to theatre, narrative, music, text, and issues of subjectivity, performance and performativity, corporeality, and the body as site of conflicting discourses.[2]

I believe Snaith's work sets out to challenge the formal boundaries placed between dance and theatre and she creates a particular environment to accomodate physical energies and kinetic movement. She concerns herself with colour, surface, texture, sound and physical interplay in the space. In this way she asserts the application of the senses throughout her processes. Like the "dance theatre" of Pina Bausch, who "broadened the concept of dance, releasing the term 'choreography' from its narrower definition as a series of connected movements"[3], Snaith's "theatredance" can be considered "theatre of experience":

> a theatre that by means of direct confrontation made reality, communicated in an aesthetic form, tangible as physical reality.[4]

For the purposes of this chapter, I will accept and respect Snaith's own classification of her work as "theatredance", while acknowledging the slippery boundaries between classifications and the usefulness of other terms. For instance, Norbert Servos identifies a lack of pretence in "dance theatre" which is fundamental to the analysis of Snaith's work:

> The performers are not 'pretending', but rather live through the experience as it is actually happening. For the audience, the act of watching is transformed into the act of witnessing. The work insists on reality being not simply represented, but experienced.[5]

Similarly, one can consider Snaith's work in relation to that of Lloyd Newson, director of DV8 Physical Theatre, who has crafted a form of physical theatre that concerns itself with current social and political realities. His performers are physically and vocally engaged in the exploration to ensure that individual perspectives are shared. The movement vocabulary is carefully chosen to reflect the meanings and intentions of common contemporary gestures and voices. Newson's intention is not to provoke or

Yolande Snaith Theatredance in Diction (1993/94). Photograph: Chris Nash.

upset an audience. He prefers to foster a questioning, reflective attitude in response to the performers' investigations. Each member of the audience is encouraged to define his/her own position in response to the work. The performances discourage passivity and encourage audiences to take on some level of responsibility, to engage with the material and be moved to a response.

Snaith is generating performance work by exploring the body-text-theatre dynamic. She creates an environment for physical and kinetic movement in response to the set and costume design, concerning herself with colour, surface and texture, as well as establishing a dialectic relationship between choreography and musical score. While often working in response to music, her dancers' rhythm and internal phrasing also creates a production's musicality. This is paralleled with the physical and dynamic qualities which the performers explore spatially and kinetically. One can certainly apply Norbert Servos's statement that "dance theatre does not anaesthetise the senses, it sharpens them for that which 'really is' ".[6] I believe Snaith's theatredance carries the potential for her audience to witness and experience the reality she creates because they can hear it, feel it and see it .

Recent Work: Research and Development
Yolande Snaith trained at Dartington College of Arts from 1979 to 1983, where her teachers were Mary Fulkerson, Steve Paxton, Rosemary Butcher, Miranda Tufnell and Julyen Hamilton, with Richard Alston also acting as external assessor. In the 1980s, the

Yolande Snaith Theatredance in Gorgeous Creatures (1998). Photograph: Chris Nash.

Arts Council began offering Research and Development (R&D) grants to enable choreographers to adequately prepare new work. This time for research before going into the studio provides an artist with an opportunity to explore the viability of initial ideas. During the two week period of R&D for *Swinger*, Snaith and actor Hassani Shapi selected sections from the book *A Lovers Discourse* by Roland Barthes as a starting point for the work. Through a deconstruction of the text, they formed a narrative, not by literally defining characters and roles, but by exploring the performers' psychological journeys. Previously, Snaith's pieces focussed more on purely physical exploration; for *Swinger*, she used text and its meaning to inform the choreographic material.

The Research and Development for *Gorgeous Creatures* in 1998 explored the concept of alter egos. Snaith chose to perform in it with an all-male cast. In the auditions, the men seemed particularly strong and somewhat idiosyncratic which Snaith considered useful features for the absurd and rather nonsensical qualities she wished to embed in the piece. While playing with various costumes and developing Snaith's relationship with the male performers through the exploration of alter egos, a costume designer suggested that the piece should be located in the Elizabethan period. Following further research, Snaith realised that she could identify with Elizabeth I and perceived that the Queen had probably sacrificed her own sexuality in order to remain powerful in her position amongst men. Snaith also saw great visual potential in this historical period regarding the set and costume design.

While Snaith's characterization became further defined and central to the structure of the piece, the other performers played between different personae and costuming, thus enabling the narrative to be fluid and non-specific, allowing the interplay of the performative elements to construct their own meaning. Lines from Shakespeare were de-constructed and then re-constructed in a nonsensical fashion and it is through this process of fragmenting the text that Snaith immobilised the words. They became part of the kinetic forces that drove the stage reality, a surreal environment imbued with an 'Alice in Wonderland' quality.

For *Blind Faith* (1999), based on the work of Leonardo da Vinci, Snaith researched the artist's life, the visual material of his contemporaries, the historical period and its scientific developments. During the Renaissance, experiments were being undertaken in the dissection of the human body. This same fascination is held by many contemporary artists today, who are exploring themes derived from such experiments. Religion was a central theme of the piece, raising questions of faith and belief, the meaning of life and death, fear of dying and losing loved ones. Working with such universal issues, it was inevitable that Snaith's dancers defined their own positions in relation to them. Handling the material from a personal perspective allows each dancer to engage with it, to find individual responses which then generate sources of imagery and a conglomerate of personal kinetic forces. This process of engagement experienced by each dancer ensures individual contributions and self-empowerment. It allows for change and personal development, transformations which provide the creative energy embedded in the work.

The question of empirical meaning certainly arises for some spectators. One reviewer wrote that "the show is theatrically satisfying but the problem is where and why the piece is going" and concluded that "I am not sure what she is saying".[7] Snaith affirms that her aim is never to tell a story. This is not to say that her work contains no structure and tension, but that the material is moulded and constructed by an intuitive sense of performative necessity rather than narrative. Seen in the context of a phenomenological perspective which proposes that phenomena can never be perceived from a static unchanging perspective but rather exist through time, I would apply Sondra Fraleigh's concept of motion when attempting to 'understand' Snaith's work:

> the essence of the dance is not identical with its motion, it arises in consciousness as the motion reveals the intent of the whole and its parts.[8]

Here consciousness is seen to unify our experience of the phenomena, and meaning and perception is in response to those parts which operate integratively to form the whole.

Snaith states clearly that the forms she creates with her performers will not deliver 'answers' as this is incompatible with the process of creation. Rather, the work intends to draw connections from the viewers' sensory perceptions. It seems that she would require all our senses to be operational and awake in order to receive such work. While not seeking a comparison, Snaith cites the work of artist Marc Chagall in an attempt to explain her work. Many images are juxtaposed within one picture and the viewer's response will be not only to its literal content but to the overall composition of visual codes in which colour, texture, design and movement create a tension in the space shared by inverted, topsy-turvy imagery.

Yolande Snaith in Conversation

I interviewed Snaith on 14 January 1999 at the Toynbee Hall in London. As the focus of my enquiry is Snaith's creative practice and processes as a choreographer, I felt it was important to discuss the following: the working relationship between choreographer/director and the performers; how performance material is devised and constructed; the nature of collaborative work; choreographic intention and personal development; and, past and present influences.

Ruth Way:

> Considering your own practice and research, what influences in terms of teaching and philosophy are impacting upon the work and its processes?

Yolande Snaith:

> Certainly Ruth Zapora and Julyen Hamilton. I trained with Ruth Zapora in Germany and Italy and many dancers who have trained in contact release attend her workshops to develop other performance skills. However, in the work she discourages contact and release for there is a different focus. She has developed a practice that is very Buddhist in nature and philosophy. It is a psychological training, a de-training, a process of letting go, stripping away all conditions and conditioning that affects the mind. This allows a pure state to emerge, a Buddhist state. During my study in contact release with Mary Fulkerson at Dartington she would take us through a meditation where we were asked to imagine clouds passing while focusing on the breath and to arrive at a completely blue sky, this being a metaphor for total clarity where distortions, walls, inhibitions and fears dissolve. I feel there is a strong connection between the release work and the Buddhist perspective. How they work with these principles is entirely different, of course, and Zapora's work is very expressive with substantial physical tension. There is no correct technique taught but you are encouraged to trust and listen to what comes out of these processes, to be exposed, naked and bare. Julyen Hamilton does a similar thing and there are several congruent factors residing in their individual approaches. He creates very specific structures and exercises that cleverly tune you into a particular aspect of improvising, to exercise a particular note/function in terms of the body. These exercises are continually evolving and come out of his understanding of improvisation, the influences from his practice in aikido, release and his own artistic sensibility. Also, on reflection, when I look back at my training at Dartington I now realise that Peter Hulton who taught writing for theatre had a large impact on my thinking and development and how I perceive theatre.

R. W.:

> How do you devise and then construct movement?

Y. S.:

> I will 'workshop' certain ideas; that is, to set improvisational tasks which require the dancer to experiment such as giving impulses, focusing on touching or the concept of manipulation. I often ask dancers to remember a pathway of movement or a series of

impulses. This is done by repetition acknowledging that what was spontaneous before, can't be again. So things are always allowed to change, to be found again, but with a difference. In *Blind Faith*, we actually filmed the improvisations and then tried to learn them from the video, but in the re-doing some moments can be easily reconstructed whereas others have to be adapted for the linking and cannot be kinetically deciphered. They're already removed from the real event. I've always regarded improvisation as a separate process used for experimentation and generating material and the choreographic skill is to mould it, shape it, and place it to serve the whole.

R.W.:

The repeating in this sense then evolves into a process of defining the material because the more familiar the dancers become with it, the physical body will remember how it arrived there. Defining the 'how' discovers how the material is linked.

Y.S.:

Yes, the dancers make sense of the their material finding the appropriate links and this develops into choreographic material which I can then direct further by an editing process, adding or taking away, changing the rhythm or spatial relationship.

R.W.:

It would seem the tasks you give are always quite specific and the limitation or, we might say, focus encourages greater development and physical understanding of the material being explored. In my experience, it's always so easy to digress or to leave material at the moment when we feel that nothing else can be found but, in fact, these are the moments which can reveal another layer of meaning and connect the performer more deeply with the material. It appears that in the process of exploration, the medium begins to embody the ideas. Would you agree?

Y.S.:

Most definitely. For *Blind Faith*, the solos grew out of a mapping task where the dancers were asked to improvise with some set material and were given a specific spatial structure to follow. By repeatedly following these pathways, the dancers would begin to recall at which points certain material would keep occurring and this became a process for defining exactly what took place on the journey. At specific points and in certain directions, the movement would locate itself to provide a spatial relationship. This created a spatial tension and a focus for the dynamics inherent in the movement.

R.W.:

Do you leave the dancers to work choreographically on a particular section?

Y.S.:

Yes. This is happening more and more now since I am finding dancers who suit my working process. I think the technical and creative training being offered today is infinitely stronger and addresses a more extensive movement vocabulary, incorporating many of the elements that originated in the New Dance era [9]: skills in contact release, use of floor, trust, weight and gravity, also the roles of symbolism, imagery and gesture found in physical theatre. Again, there is always an editing, paring down process, rearranging material which requires the directorial eye and choreographer's sensibility to facilitate the emerging form.

R.W.:

Could you talk about the dancers' contribution to the collaborative process?

Y.S.:

This has certainly become more important and, as you know, I do acknowledge their choreographic contribution in the programme. As my work has progressed, I have become very disinterested in creating movement sequences for dancers and feeling the need to control the material. I wanted to work with differences and different movement vocabularies and I have found this expansion very satisfying and intriguing to direct. When dancers invest in the work, they have a greater connection with it and I have noticed a stronger commitment because of this.

R.W.:

As a performer myself, I am interested in that sense of empowerment that comes from being able to contribute to the creation, the vision. It would seem that the collaborative process would depend on the working relationship between the director and performers and also the chemistry between the dancers themselves. The improvisational processes you set up necessitate an openness and create an environment for the dancers to explore, likewise the moulding, crafting of material realises the potential in performer and medium. I think acknowledgement that both facilitate each other is very positive and, in the sense of responding and nurturing choreographic talent, very important to those involved and the performance outcome.... The music composed by Graeme Miller for *Blind Faith* offered many contrasting sections regarding style, tempo and mood. How does he work alongside your process?

Y.S.:

It's very interesting. Graeme is now regularly composing for dance but when we first met he wasn't that interested and I had to be very persuasive. In fact, we don't discuss music, we discuss the psychology of the piece, the atmosphere and the energy in the space. It allows him a creative space to tune into, an emotional response, and musical terms here seem inadequate. He's the musician. I let him get on with it as I get on with the choreography. Because he's worked in theatre himself, he's deeply aware of the theatrical processes and I feel this forms the basis of our working relationship, rather like a silent understanding. He is tuned into my process visually and dynamically. He is able to feel the material and where it is going. Over time through the experiences, we have honed our working relationship. In the beginning we would work in rehearsal with no music. It would arrive just before the performance deadline and it worked. But not every time, so now samples of music are played in all rehearsals giving us both the opportunity for ongoing analysis and development. I feel creating the right conditions for artists supports the creativity imbued in the work.

R.W.:

Certainly the dancers would have more time to embody the musical forms to build an interplay between the internal phrasing of the music and the inherent phrasing and dynamics of the movement. But your work also suggests a co-existence with the music where the movement doesn't depend on it, for it is clearly making independent statements. Even though at times there is interaction, these statements appear in control, so the physicality is leading, driving the intentions.

Y.S.:

Yes, the action is defined from the body and very often I have to remind the dancers to maintain their own timing and not be swayed by the music but sometimes when a sequence relies on a precise physical timing, as in catching and falling, here a musical structure can accentuate those arrival points and be very supportive. One of my pet hates is when choreography is driven only by the beat in the music for it seems to diminish the possibility to read into the event from other perspectives. It instructs us to follow rather than allowing us to use our imaginations and construct individual responses.

R.W.:

You have a long history of working with props, but I see you have moved away from using smaller objects to working with larger pieces of furniture. Could you talk about this progression?

Y.S.:

Yes. Originally the props were central to my investigations, particularly in my solo work and then duet work with Kathy Krick. This preoccupation then moved onto working with furniture. Regarding *Swinger*, with the central piece being the pendulum, I met with the designer well in advance. We were both very interested in Rebecca Horn as a conceptual artist and her work with pendulums. This stimulus took us into the theatre space to experiment with some ropes and buckets of sand and directly out of this play the designer conceived the pendulum for the show. For *Blind Faith*, the decision to have one piece of furniture that doesn't move became a new challenge and necessitated a different focus for the work. By focus I mean in handling the spacial relationships and movement. In fact, for my next piece I am looking to create a space, a chamber with no objects. This is the ultimate challenge for me as I have used these things to provide me with a method of working that doesn't fall into the traditions and expectations of dance.

Conclusion: Phenomenal Dancers and Collaboration

It is apparent that Snaith is not only honing her choreographic craft through ongoing committed practice but has sought out the potential in the collaborative aspects inherent in her work. Here we must recognise that Snaith chooses to work with performers, composers and designers who are best suited to her working methods.

These are artists skilled in improvisation and the performers could be described as "phenomenal dancers". According to Valerie Preston-Dunlop,

> the phenomenal dancer is never an object moving to commands but lives every movement, a phenomenal dancer creates every movement for s/he turns an instruction into a creation.[10]

In Snaith's work, the performers' input is integral to the process and the outcome.

As a director and choreographer, Snaith values her artists as creative thinkers and technique is embedded into the creative processes which facilitate the phenomenal experience. In this way, the physical preparation the performers execute can be perceived as an essential and vital part of the creative process where the physiological body and the senses are awakened and tuned. This preparation, or physical journey, acts then as an informer, a catalyst for creative exploration. A distinctive relationship is constructed between the technical attributes and the creative energies which require the dancer to seek out physical solutions to tasks and to construct intention and meaning in his/her own work.

Snaith's artistic development is based on rigorous physical, emotional and theoretical investigation. She is acutely aware of the need to avoid formulaic systems of working and instead reinvests in her processes to craft material in collaboration with her artists. She employs a distilling process whereby she extracts the living moment from the kinetic, aural, somatic, spatial and emotional dimensions. Snaith invites our senses to be awakened and integrated by the fusion of these elements in her theatredance.

Acknowledgement

I would like to thank Yolande for her honesty, integrity and for assisting me with this article.

Notes

1 Ana Sanchez-Colberg, 'Charting the Road Towards a Physical Theatre', in *Performance Research*, Volume 1 no. 2, Summer 1996, p. 40.

2 Rachel Duerdon and Neil Fisher, 'Dance theatre: what is it?' in *Animated*, Spring 1999, p. 36.

3 Norbert Servos, 'Pina Bausch: Dance and Emancipation' in A. Carter (ed), *The Routledge Dance Studies Reader* (London: Routledge, 1998), p. 37.

4 *ibid.*

5 *ibid.*, p. 40.

6 *ibid.*

7 Jann Parry, *The Observer*, 8 March 1998.

8 Sondra Fraleigh, 'Seeing Dance Through Phenomenology' in A. Carter (ed), *The Routledge Dance Studies Reader* (London: Routledge,1998), p. 137.

9 The term "new dance" was coined with the publication of the first issue of *New Dance Magazine* in 1977. This was a project initiated by a group of dancers who called themselves the X6 collective after their working base, X6 Dance Space in the Bermondsey Docklands, London. The collective existed from 1976 to 1980. See Stephanie Jordan, *Striding Out* (Dance Books, 1992), chapter 3, p. 58.

10 Valerie Preston-Dunlop, *Looking at Dances* (Verve Publishing,1998), p. 57.

5 Re-Cognizing Corporeality

Henry Daniel

...the continuity of any cultural phenomenon, the praxis of any body of knowledge, involves a string of people not simply learning a set of axioms which someone invented in the past, but also themselves repeating the cognitive breakthrough of its 'inventor' and actually re-inventing the institution itself each time. Any phenomenon - geometry or performance, for example - can be understood and practised only when each new member repeats the original cognitive leap.[1]

Introduction

The spectator-performer relationship is at base an interactive process; by this I mean that there are energies that automatically resonate back and forth between spectators and performers. These set the tone of the encounter and facilitate the assimilation of information. This is the main premise under which many performers/artists using new 'intelligent' systems that interact with the body in performance operate. The artist seeks to focus greater attention on dynamic processes as an interactive communication of information between spectator, performer, and performing environment. When one works closely with an art form that emphasises physical movement as its primary vocabulary, attempts to combine these movement forms with relatively sophisticated performance technologies place the individual spectator and performer in a much more complex situation that requires a different approach to the problem of awareness.

Re-cognizing corporeal being is another kind of experiencing, a remembering or retracing of certain paths which may at some time, often quite distant from the performance event, have had some role in determining embodied behaviour patterns in the individual. Its processes outline a useful means of addressing relations between embodied self and those other elements that form an important part of the performing environment but which appear 'separate from' the individual. One only need look at the model of an Internet-based performance to realise that a credible means of dealing with such events which are spread over extensive space-time locations is paramount for the audience member and participant. The relationship between silicon and "flesh and blood" is one that needs to be adequately recognised. The influence of these two substances or materials on each other is set to become more and more crucial to the performance equation. The intricate interactions between their processes, to my mind, assume a significance that by itself constitutes a new idea of the performative.

The new 'intelligent' systems to which I refer and which are used in a performance context move dancers, actors and spectators through ultrasonic and other invisible fields to create imaginative visual and sound simulacra. Interactive floors, walls, and "costumes" made of sophisticated materials electronically prepared to respond to human stimuli. Mechanical equipment of a diverse nature is worn on the body by performers; the fields of interaction that they produce allow audiences to participate more actively in performance events. Such performances can occur in several distant locations simultaneously and can be made accessible to viewers or other participants at these remote sites via the phenomenon of the World Wide Web.[2] The individual's relationship to his or her own body and the ability to respond to others, who in a sense are mediated by these technologies, is of great importance. The concept of embodied presence as a type of awareness construct which consists of all the processes that being in space-time involves is the central tenet of my argument.

Re-cognizing Corporeal Being

There are many who presently lean toward the view that the human body is in various states of evolution which will eventually make many of its functions obsolete. The Australian performance artist Stelarc is one such example.[3] He seems intent on accelerating this process through his own performance agenda and appears preoccupied with reorganizing his own physical appearance in accordance with this agenda. Stelarc is by no means singular in these beliefs. Ray Kurzweil, one of the world's foremost authorities on Artificial Intelligence believes that we are on an evolutionary path where the future of the human being lies in silicon-based rather than carbon-based bodies. He has even devised a projected timetable for this to happen. This period stretches from the birth of the Universe, 10 to 1 billion years ago (Kurzweil's estimate), to the year 2099 when there is no longer any "clear distinction between humans and computers".[4]

This climate of radical opinion regarding the current and future role of our biological bodies is partly the result of our incessant drive toward technological advancement. It is this current scientific knowledge that we possess that allows the Stelarcs and Kurzweils to make such bold claims. It is also because of this attitude that there is a large gap between what our bodies are presently capable of doing and what technology predicts that we will be able to do in the future. This gap exposes a problem regarding the predicament of live bodies interacting with technology in the performance environment. This is where the concept of re-cognizing corporeality can be useful.

I propose that any non-sentient object, electronic device, tool or material that performers directly use as extensions of themselves and/or the space itself (in short any object on which our attention becomes focussed), can influence the reorganization of interactive energies that occur during performance. These actions are performic in the sense that they are part of an interactive process which is open to creative manipulation by individual intent. If, as I am suggesting, we give 'life' and 'existence' to things through our attention, new technologies have a potential 'life' of their own that is determined by those of us who use it or acknowledge in ourselves the conditions for its use. Through such means performances can acquire a new density and complexity of references that resonate across the physical, biological and cultural institutions out of which our bodies have emerged.

There is immense room in this concept for dialogue. I will limit myself to three areas which I shall briefly outline. Firstly, there is the dialogue that one can have with 'other' aspects that are internal to oneself. This becomes possible by using one ability or function to focus on another. Secondly, one can direct this attention outwardly in a dialogical relationship with those non-sentient bodies or objects situated in the space. Thirdly and lastly, there is a deeper type of communication that becomes available to those who are witnesses or participants through the agency of the body even though they may be located at diverse and distant points to each other.

One can compare the first type of dialogue to a kind of introspective activity. The difference however is that there is no single self on which to introspect but a series of positions from which one can observe. The second type displays some important parallels with practices used by early civilisations in their 'worship' of objects as deities or gods. The power that is inherent in these acts of worship comes primarily from the attention that the 'worshipper' transfers to these objects, very much like the attention we devote to technology today. The third type concentrates on the differences between the way that people share information with each other as opposed to the way that they do so with machines. These differences are quite apparent to anyone who has ever performed with any of the new sensitive technologies.

The complex play of directed and redirected energies that occur generally during a performance I will call the performic principle; those between human sentient beings I call the performative principle. The difference lies in the element of intent that allows one to focus attention. The role of performer and spectator in this context is extremely flexible because anyone and anything can be 'on-stage' or 'in focus' at any moment depending on the manner in which one chooses to focus this attention. The individual thus has the possibility of cultivating a deeper awareness of his or her own physically embodied presence through focussing on details of the dynamic interplay that is at the heart of what we call presence.

Re-cognizing corporeal being acknowledges the individual configurations of energy that automatically attract or are repelled by other configurations which stand in relative proximity to them. As witnesses/participants, we are obliged to make sense of our actions by "composing" meanings in accordance with our own world picture. My argument claims that the much more complex levels of information with which we can interact are not always reducible to logical and meaningful narratives and that they are, in themselves, performic relations between aspects of embodied knowledge. This knowledge can be elusive to an approach that uses linear style logic. It can however become coherent with a different approach. One must however understand that the body, in the required state of preparedness, can take in and relay complex events with a degree of simultaneity that is equivalent to quantum behaviour. This concept will have many important lessons to teach us about the human condition. Manipulating the discrete mechanisms which are distributed throughout our bodies is one way of performing such changes. These articulations and manipulations set processes in motion that continue long after the physical actions themselves have been completed.

This concept is true for the performer as well as the spectator. The 'remembrance' of physical actions which are embodied in the body as bio-evolutionary is never lost, even though the duration and strength of its 'recall' may vary. These innate processes can be set in motion through physical, mental, emotional and psychic processes. In a sense, new versions of reality can be witnessed, and the possibility of entering into other people's versions is a distinct possibility. Yoga techniques are examples of this process; physical manipulation of the body sets up complex re-cognitive processes whereby the body 'remembers' its own history, or more accurately the history of processes that it has undergone at the genetic and cultural level. Through intent, attention and awareness can be projected throughout and beyond our corporeal frames. In many ways technology forces us to pay attention to these processes. When we do, we are reminded of the possibilities we have for embodying and becoming embodied with.

Some Comparative Approaches

Most mainstream scientists today seem to favour a brain-centred model in the general debate on consciousness. Such an approach tends to marginalize the importance of the corporeal, something that is of such crucial importance to the performing artist. Leder, in his book *The Absent Body*, makes a good attempt to redress this situation by focusing on the ways in which bodies literally become absent in regular day-to-day activities. As a performing artist myself, I am extremely sympathetic to approaches of this kind. Leder argues that "The body is capable of incorporating within its phenomenological domain objects that remain spatially discrete".[5] He goes on to cite an example used by Heidegger of the tool as a "ready to hand (*zuhanden*), part of an equipment structure that tends to withdraw from our explicit attention" through its use. This physical connection of the body with the tool, its extension through another object or person, and the attempt to influence or communicate with a distant entity has a familiar ring. The analogies with new "intelligent" or "sensitive" technologies is evident. One imbues the technology as tool with a significance that indeed cannot be withdrawn from our explicit attention. Leder is not a man of the theatre, but his arguments open a way forward for the insertion of a theatrical element within his discourse.

Francis Crick, in a book he subtitles *The Scientific Search for the Soul*, offers another model in which he attempts to lay a scientific foundation for the mystery of consciousness itself. In a series of arguments he states quite categorically that everything in our patterns of behaviour can be reduced to the physical operations of the cerebral mind-brain.

> The scientific belief is that our minds – the behaviour of our brains – can be explained by the interaction of nerve cells (and other cells) and the molecules associated with them.[6]

Crick sets up his main argument with this statement and concludes with a similar one.

> The language of the brain is based on neurons. To understand the brain you must understand neurons and especially how vast numbers of them act together in parallel.[7]

Crick has little to say about free will and this is relegated to a couple of pages in a postscript at the end of the work. He claims that free will is merely an ability to make decisions (his examples include verbal responses and physical movement actions) which are controlled by a region "in or near" the "anterior singulate sulcus" of the brain, which is itself a region that receives "many inputs from the higher sensory regions" and is "at or near the higher levels of the motor system".[8] Crick's implication is that decision making is completely different from and not to be confused with free will. Movement actions and verbal responses may belong to the higher sensory system but they are in effect automatically playing out deeply programmed information at the genetic level. While Crick's arguments might seem quite compelling, they do not take into account something that I believe is essential to the nature of performance; that is, the fact that it is a process that requires much more than automatic interactive nerve communications.

The means whereby these nerve interactions are set in motion may be automatic, but without a level of individual intent, the process of true creativity cannot begin. When performances are successful, there is always evidence of awareness being consciously manipulated. The processes, the physical paths traversed, and the methods used, are of utmost importance. Theatrical 'experiments' by movement artists featuring bodies involved in these dynamic processes are more than states of automatic cerebral activity. They are also not simply performic. Performances by dancers, actors and spectators can achieve more power when informed by personal experience and guided by individual intent. These are holistic events in that complex systems perform complex operations in a whole that is not reducible to the sum of its individual parts.

Crick claims that "the aim of science is to explain *all* aspects of the behaviour of our brains, including those of musicians, mystics, and mathematicians".[9] If his science implies that one must achieve a set of repeatable and verifiable results from a set of inferences or hypotheses, then theatre can be scientific. However if the terms 'exact' and 'verifiable' mean measurable in an empirical sense, such definitions will exclude much of what is the essence of performance. In the theatre, positive results depend as much on an individual's personal power and charisma as much as on the willingness and preparedness of the spectator to participate in the reality of their actions. Personal power and charisma necessitates an ability to manipulate awareness, the nature of which is subject to the principles of quantum indeterminacy. One can be aware of, witness, and even accept the results of performance without fully being able to logically and coherently explain why. My argument claims that this level of understanding can occur only after the individual has re-cognized important aspects of their own experiences as these resonate with the immediate performance.

"Metakinetic Transfer"

A concept that is related to re-cognizing corporeality and worthy of note has previously been offered by John Martin (1893–1985), dance critic for *The New York Times* from 1927 to 1962. Martin's close relationship with theatre, especially the early modern dance movement in America, enabled him to develop, at first hand, a concept that promised to "explain those things for which words are not adequate".[10] His "metakinetic transfer" is important in an historical context. The degree to which technology and dance interacts is probably much more intense today than in Martin's time, but he nevertheless approached the idea of communication through movement and of awakening certain perceptions through dance in a manner that has been helpful to my investigations. For Martin, movement was in and of itself "a medium for the transference of an aesthetic and emotional concept from the consciousness of one individual to that of another". He states:

> There is correlated with kinesis a supposed psychic accompaniment called metakinesis, this correlation growing from the theory that the physical and the psychical are merely two aspects of a single underlying reality.[11]

Martin's argument is that there is a component to our awareness of being that can only be expressed through physical movement and this awareness can be communicated from one person to the other without individual physical contact. However, the kinds of dance about which Martin wrote favourably had a substantial emotive appeal which may have fuelled his idea of kinetic transfer. In his distrust of other kinds of dance that did not rely on this heavy emotional input (e.g. Merce Cunningham's work), he exposes a hesitance and a conservatism that I find in retrospect quite interesting.

Martin seemed to be drawn toward a powerful emotional expressiveness in the work of Martha Graham for instance. Some of her early and better known works like *Appalachian Spring* (1944), about life on the early American frontier, and *Clytemnaestra* (1958), a work on the tragedy of Medea in ancient Greece, are good examples of this. These pieces had the stuff of epic drama, where the individual spirit battled on important thresholds, in danger of being overrun by hostile forces. It is not difficult to imagine the determination, strong physical presence, and iron-clad intent that this kind of work needed, and which did not fail to impress audiences then and now.

The works of Merce Cunningham and his main collaborator John Cage, for example, were of a completely different sort altogether. These men were the harbingers of the postmodern in dance. Here dramatic narratives were non-existent and irrelevant. Processes however were of utmost importance. The body was most importantly not so much the site of individual suffering as a place to observe the workings of these processes as interactions of energy. As a result of this approach, a great deal of abstraction came into play. The plastic arts, especially painting, also played an important role. The approach to music, if one could call some of Cage's experiments as such, was another matter altogether. Perhaps experimental electronic sound media may be one of the labels one could attach to Cage's work. Generally speaking, it appeared that Cunningham and his collaborators made every attempt to dissociate themselves from the more traditional modes of making and perceiving theatrical dance. This of course necessitated a change in the way one could analyze the role the individual should play in re-cognizing the performance.

Martin was obviously extremely sceptical of these ideas. He himself had directed theatrical productions early in his career around the time when Stanislavsky and the Moscow Art Theatre were making their incursions into the American theatre scene. The dictum for the actor to be "true" to the role was ever present then. The new directions that were appearing in the works of Cunningham and Cage were quite different and opposite to what was available. Theirs and Graham's work indicate two different approaches to the concept of meaning in the choreographic form itself. Their methods point to the embodying and unravelling of different layers of content. Although one can attempt to isolate, reassess, and stage kinetic and emotive aspects apart from and in parallel to each other, the fact is that this cannot happen without loss to the whole. In other words we will always consciously miss something. One needs to continually step aside from one way of looking and seeing in order to have a more complete picture. This complete picture exists in itself and as itself but more often than not we do not see it as such. In a sense these two choreographers represent two diametrically opposed views, both of which help to identify a more complete picture. In my opinion the difficulty that Martin had in accepting the approach of the postmodern was directly related to his own reliance on the emotive-narrative link as a means of individual re-cognition.

Martin's concept of "metakinesis", "kinetic transfer" or "kinaesthetic response",[12] a kind of "inner mimicry" which made it possible for the spectator to apprehend the dance on its own physical terms was dependent on a strong emotional power that the early modern dance relied on. This can encourage an audience to become lazy participants. These powerful energies can also distract from other means of apprehension. As a result certain aspects of the communicative dialogue suffers. Martin and others who witnessed these works may have sat eagerly waiting to be transported into realms of kinetic and emotional excitement. Closeness to this kind of energy stimulates and excites but, like gladiatorial-style games, it can absolve the audience from taking personal risk and responsibility.

Although Martin himself has written that "Movement is the most elementary physical experience of human life,"[13] he also implies that this movement should be expressive of a particular aspect of the human condition. There is a substantial shift in contemporary work with the advent of new technologies. However now, as in Martin's time, the individual and his/her ability to continually redefine their relationship to corporeal presence is crucial. Relationships of movement to sound, image to movement, and both in relation to our total sensual environment, emphasizes the cross-referencing of modes of realization which in turn influence who we are and what we can become. Dance and movement theatre need additional layers of discourse that Martin is not able to provide.

Conclusion

Although outdated, Martin's ideas still have some relevance to movement theatre work produced today. They certainly point us in the right direction in terms of formulating expanded notions of the role that individuals can play in re-cognizing corporeal being. My approach is intended to encourage individual understanding of the complexity of the performance event and to apprehend it *as it occurs*, even though one may not understand its implications via the linear logical method. The event or chain of events can be re-cognized because they are embodied; that is, they are stored at different layers of the body. The layers are located in psychic activity, mental activity and emotional activity, all inseparable from physical movement processes. Without the experience that our fleshly bodies are capable of recording, none of the manifestations of these other layers would be apparent. In other words, our bodies are the receptors and transmitters for complex manifestations of natural and cosmic phenomena, on which we can have some level of influence.

Embodiment is an holistic event that is subject to quantum behaviour, meaning that events happen simultaneously and can be apprehended as such. It is our linear logic that forces us to decide on only a few aspects of the complex event we are always within. Simultaneity and complexity is part of our natural state of being. Selectivity is decision making and is an acquired function with specific aims dictated by prevailing norms. While I propose that theatre is the place where one can use intent to play one mode against the other, re-cognition is the strategic mode through which spectator and performer can re-cognize themselves within a performance. This can be an important key to understanding being and a technique that can clarify the role that verbal and written language plays in determining realities. Also, as I mentioned earlier, performance is one of the fundamental modes of stepping outside our acquired everyday behaviour and restoring other levels of coherency to our being.

Notes

1   D. George, 'Performance Epistemology' in *Performance Research* Vol. 1 no. 1, 1996, p. 17.

2   See H. Daniel and O. Taiwo, 'Shango meets Ogun', in conjunction with The Global Café. Choreography archived at http://gold.globalcafe.co.uk, 1999.

3   See http://www.stelarc.va.com.au/ for performance extracts.

4   R. Kurzweil, *The Age of Spiritual Machines* (London: Orion Business Books, 1999), pp. 261-280.

5   D. Leder, *The Absent Body* (Chicago and London: The University of Chicago Press, 1990), p. 33.

6   F. Crick, *The Astonishing Hypothesis* (London: Simon and Schuster, 1994 ed), p. 7.

7   *ibid.,* p. 256.

8   *ibid.,* p. 267.

9   *ibid.,* p. 259.

10 J. Martin, *The Modern Dance* (New York: AS Barnes, 1933/1965 ed), p. 13.

11 *ibid.,* p. 14

12 J. Martin, *Introduction to the Dance* (New York: Dance Horizons, 1978 ed).

13 J. Martin, *The Modern Dance,* pp. 7-8.

6 Conventionalization
the Soul of *Jingju*

Ruru Li & David W. Jiang

Jingju,[1] known as Peking Opera in the West, is one of over three hundred regional theatres existing in China today. Long regarded as the characteristic form of the traditional Chinese theatre,[2] it did not in fact start taking shape until two hundred years ago, but soon developed into a unique form by absorbing various theatrical elements from other genres. In 1790, Emperor Qianlong of the Qing dynasty ordered some *huiju* troupes (local theatre from the Anhui area) to come to Beijing for the celebration of his eightieth birthday. These troupes brought to the Palace and ordinary Beijing audiences new melodies, acrobatic movements and a wider range of repertoire. They stayed in the capital and recruited more performers from other genres like *qinqiang* (Melody of Qin)[3] as well as *kunqu* or *kunju*[4] that had dominated the Chinese stage for the previous two hundred years. The impact of the blending of actors from different genres was influential in the development of Chinese theatre, since it radically affected the theatre circles in the capital, and it paved the way for *jingju*'s emergence. A few years later, more troupes came from the southern region along the middle reaches of the Yangtze River bringing with them the Melody of Han (*handiao*) and both performers and their melodies were soon assimilated by the rising theatre of *jingju*.

As a new theatrical form, *jingju* was based on its many predecessors, and its artistic features gradually formed by transforming and evolving from other genres. When *jingju* became mature, other younger regional theatres started using its techniques and skills in their own development. Furthermore, the old genres on which *jingju* was based now also borrowed from it in order to compete with other newly-born regional theatres. The traditional Chinese theatre comprises more than three hundred local theatrical forms which overlap and interact with each other. Within this complex system, *jingju* holds a very special position, for apart from the early support it received from the court, it served as a link between the past and the new genres of the future. More importantly, when it first appeared, it was an innovative form and it won out over *kunju*, then the dominant theatre, by reason of its "vulgar" flavour as well as its bold characteristic of hybridizing different genres. Absorbing features from other theatres, *jingju* established its own system, which later underwent various changes from radical to conservative, flexible to rigid, as well as from new to old.

Conventionalization, a term coined by Zhao Taimou in 1927, is the key to understanding the system.[5] This means that in *jingju* there are certain moods, patterns or rules that practitioners have to follow. It is also the aesthetic principle for *jingju* that has decided the style of the performance, the position of the performers, and their relationship with the spectators as well. The concept is best demonstrated by acting, because, above all, *jingju* is a theatre whose "stories are uttered in the form of song and dance".[6] The definition, formulated by Wang Guowei at the beginning of this century after his scrupulous study of both Chinese and Western theatres, covers a wide range of performing aspects: singing, reciting, acting and dance (including martial arts) – the four basic skills that a *jingju* actor has to master. When they are all blended together with the accompaniment of music and percussion, the conception of acting in *jingju* is framed. Acting is in bold relief against a light background of other theatrical elements of the genre, and therefore an attempt to investigate how conventionalization dominates and guides acting may serve as an approach to grasping the essence of this theatrical form.

Mei Lanfang, an internationally renowned master of *jingju* (1894-1961), once explained the idea of conventionalization as follows:

> Each character type has certain acting rules to conform to. In general these can be divided into five categories [relating to human being's body]: mouth (singing and reciting), eyes, hands, steps and body.... These rules also represent basic skills. Each character type must have strict training first, and when s/he is on the stage, his/her voice and body movements, accompanied by music and percussion, become an integral whole that accurately expresses different inner feelings of the characters in the play. These rules should not be performed in a mechanical way merely displaying all types of techniques. Instead, they should be combined organically, and should take account of the differing demands of different role types. They are the creations on the stage.[7]

Acting on the *jingju* stage is first of all conditioned by the character type of roles. Different role types have their own way of speaking, singing, walking, gesturing or dancing.

There are basically four role types: *sheng* (male part), *dan* (female part), *jing* (male painted-face) and *chou* (the clown). Each role type has its own sub-types; for example, there are old, young and martial *sheng*. Even within the martial *sheng*, the sub-type can be further divided into the one with armour and one without armour. The division of roles is based on sex, age and performing speciality.[8] For instance, the *laodan* (old woman part) is for old women, while the *qingyi* (literally black gown woman part) is for a young to middle-aged woman. Both types demand good singing skills, but the former uses natural voice and the latter the high-pitched falsetto voice, which is also used in all the other female roles demonstrating the femininity. The origin of the exaggerated representation of the female voice is doubtless also related to the fact that female roles were once universally played by male impersonation. For young women, there is another character role – the *huadan* (literally, flowery woman part portraying vigorous young women like maids or daughters from a poor background or women who are lascivious). Acting and reciting are more important for the *huadan*. There are also different sub-types of woman warriors. In *jingju*, each sub-type of character role has different schools based on the style of singing and acting of the master who was the founder of the particular school. Generally speaking, there are five famous schools for the young female part [9] and four for the old male part. Other character types also have their own schools of singing and acting. Each school has its own repertoire and the same play can be performed by different schools in different styles.

Different character types wear different make-up and costumes, which are essential assistance for acting. The wide variety of make-up ranges from the old male/female part who wears flesh-coloured paint, to the young male/female part who has a white forehead, nose and chin as well as pink cheeks and eye-lids. The *jing* character type, the painted face, uses about four hundred patterns.[10] For male and female parts, eyes and eyebrows are painted a raven black colour. The end of eyes and eyebrows are then lifted by means of a head band worn very tight around the skull. This gives a startling effect and highlights the expressions which can be seen by audiences even at the back of the square or a large auditorium. This part of the face has always been a focus of Chinese visual arts, and exaggerating the shape of eyes and eyebrows has served as a way to emphasize them. The *jing* is often a character type known more for courage and resourcefulness than for scholarly intelligence.[11] Different colours for the *jing*'s facial patterns are usually symbolic: red often symbolizes goodness, loyalty and bravery; black is for a character who is honest, straightforward and upright; watery white stands for cruelty and treachery while oily white denotes an inflated domineering

person. Blue often indicates some bandit sort of background of the characters, gold and silver are used on the faces and bodies of deities, spirits and the Buddha, while green suggests a ghostly quality.

Colour is also associated with the shape of the facial patterns. For example, the Hegemon King of Chu in *Farewell My Concubine* (*Ba wang bie ji*) is a tragic hero. He is brave on the battlefields, but lacks strategic wisdom; he has courage but is arrogant. The dominating colours of his painted face are black and white with his eyes and eyebrows going down (see Figure 1). This is the facial expression of weeping which conveys his fate and failure in his life. The Chinese clown often has a white patch on his nose, but the patterns of the patches may be in the shape of butterfly wings or round or triangular. The different shape of the patches tells the audience if the clown is good or evil.

Linked with the make-up, there are glamorous costumes, based on the Ming dynasty's styles but with variations introduced for the sake of acting effect. For example, the "water-sleeves" (flimsy white sleeves about two feet long), the

Figure 1. The facial pattern of the Hegemon King of Chu in Farewell My Concubine. Performed by DW Jiang

essential means for gestures and dances in *jingju*, were a transformation of the voluminous sleeves ancient people wore in everyday life. Sometimes Qing-dynasty-style costumes are also used. All costumes are made from silk, and embroidered with bright coloured patterns. There are strict rules for the style, colour and patterns a character should wear. An emperor must wear an apricot coloured gown embroidered with dragons, the sun and the sea, while the queen's clothes are often decorated with a phoenix image. Costumes are not made according to roles of the specific play but decided either by the status (kings and queens in any period wear similar costumes) or by the character types. For example, the *qingyi* usually wears a full-length gown with long flimsy sleeves, while the *huadan* is often dressed in trousers and jacket, sometimes with a skirt or an apron. It is interesting to note that the beggar is attired in a special gown. This is again made from silk patched with silk in various colours. The patches are supposed to indicate that the gown has been mended, revealing the character's poverty.[12]

Both make-up and costumes are largely decorative. They denote the identity of the roles, and also play a meaningful role in acting. There are many special techniques, skills and coded sets that an actor needs to master concerning the water-sleeves, beard, hair, hats, fans, handkerchiefs, etc.. For instance, Cheng Yanqiu, one of the great *dan* masters, created ten different methods of using the water sleeves in order to express different feelings and emotions, such as anger, surprise, shock, excitement, anxiety, and despair.[13]

As defined by Wang Guowei, song and dance serve to tell the story, and therefore music, especially the singing of arias, is the most important theatrical element in this form. Again, it is conventionalized. There are basically three styles of musical patterns (*xipi, erhuang* and *fan erhuang*) which have strict prosodic rules with rhythm and rhymes, but vary according to mood. Lyrics are fitted into specific musical sentences. All the three basic patterns originated from the other theatrical genres which were the foundation of *jingju* two hundred years ago, and the melodies for each style are also restricted to a set pattern. *Jingju* has no composer in the Western sense. In former times, the music of the aria, which often consisted of variations on the basis of the original style, was worked out between the *huqin* (the main string instrument) player and the leading performers. During the last thirty or so years, composers have been responsible for the music of newly written librettos, but their job is more or less the same as described above.

The essential rule regarding gestures and body movements is the general balance of the body, while arms and hands should always be displayed in curved and rounded movements. There are many sets for each character type, and these can take the form of a two to ten minute solo dance, or a group dance, or fighting between two people or two groups. These sets range from preparation for the first appearance on the stage to fighting in a battle, riding a horse, rowing a boat, action in the dark and sewing; or the use of beard, hat, feather plumes or water-sleeves in order to express certain feelings or emotions. They include complicated acrobatics, using chairs, tables and ancient weapons as well as simple stylized mime, such as walking upstairs or downstairs, opening or closing a door, looking at a person or gazing into the distance, etc.. There are also clearly regulated movements for fingers, fists, arms, feet, legs and eyes, and all these conventions are included by Mei's five categories when he discussed acting in *jingju*. The function of conventionalization in this area is similar to that of the musical notes. *Jingju* has hundreds of minute units of gestures and body movements, and each has its precise rules to conform to. But when differing units are combined, a new series will appear, and the resulting creations thus become endless. Stanislavsky, after seeing one of Mei Lanfang's performances in Moscow in 1935, was impressed by this strange and fascinating combination of "limitation and freedom". He commented that the acting on the Chinese stage is made up of "free movements with rules".[14]

Conventionalization hence no longer means the mere equivalent of formulae or rules; it also mirrors the aesthetic principles of *jingju*. Speaking, gestures and body movements are no longer simple imitations of real life, but become singing or dance with accurate rhythms accompanied by set music and percussion. Many research works are dedicated to the practice of acting. For instance, Kowzan once made a division between auditive and visual signs in the performing system in order to explore the centrality of the actor. In his work, he argued that the auditive signs relate directly to the actor, while the visual signs are generated outside the actor. If we use Kowzan's idea as a starting point, a *jingju* actor's tasks become doubly more difficult, for both auditive and visual signs on the stage only acquire those specific meanings that an actor's performance bestow on them.

We can take props, part of the visual signs, as an example. Associated with the decorative and stylized make-up and costumes, props on the stage are also highly decorated and often different from their originals in everyday life. A horse whip does not look anything like a real one: it is made from a stick about a foot long wound round with heavy silk tassels in different colours – blue, green, yellow or even purple. The whip is supposed to represent the colour of the horse, but in most cases it matches the colour of the costumes worn by the performers. Such an object, completely different from a prop in the realistic theatre in the West, means nothing at all if it stands simply on its own. But, when it is further coded by the performance of the actor (for instance, when his/her leg kicks up as if mounting a horse, or when s/he jumps, somersaults and makes other acrobatic movements), the tasselled stick is not only transformed into a horse whip, but also into a horse. Similarly, guided by the performers, such transformations can easily take place between an oar and a boat, green flags and sea waves, as well as red flags and fire. The use of props on the *jingju* stage demonstrates that all the signs employed in this theatre have to be encoded by the performers' own bodies and physical movements. Scenery is no exception.

Flexibility of space and time is another remarkable feature of *jingju*. For instance, characters may have been at court a moment ago, but after walking around the stage once, the scene has immediately turned into a battle field or any other place. An empty space of the stage can be the bank of a river, however, when the boatman appears with an oar in his hands, his gestures, movements and dance immediately lead audiences to understand that the scene has changed and that the location is now on the river. All these examples illustrate the basic idea of scenography in *jingju*: "The scenery changes whenever the actor moves".

Furthermore, performers are the real creators of a performance text. In *jingju*, apart from reciting, none of the remaining components of this "total theatre"[15] like singing, acting, dance and martial arts can be represented by a written form. Thus, a written script is quite different from what is presented on the stage. We can take *Picking up the Jade Bracelet* (Shi yu zhuo)[16] as an example. This is a short play about two young people falling in love at first sight. The girl is from a lower-class family and she helps her mother to raise chickens. After coming on the stage, the girl introduces herself and her situation to the audience. "Zi bao jia men" or "self-reporting about one's household/identity" is the convention in playwriting for the first appearance of each leading character in a play. Then the script continues as follows:

Sun Yujiao:

I must now let the chicks out and do some embroidery at the door.

[*sings*]   It is lovely spring weather outside; the sun is shining and the breeze is gentle; One stitch up and one stitch down, I am passing time doing my embroidery.

However, when actually performed, there is a fifteen-minute scene before the girl starts her aria after her speech. She first performs a mime showing how to get the chicks out, then discovers that there is one missing. Having found the missing one, she then feeds the chicks, but unfortunately gets some of the husk into her eye. After the "feeding chicken scene", she then takes a chair to the front stage, and sits down to prepare her embroidery work. She compares different coloured threads, and then puts the thin thread through the eye of the needle. Of course, this is again a set of mimes and gestures, and only then, does the written script resume.

The example above shows that in *jingju*, the written script only provides a very little part of the whole future creative work on the stage. Although the playwriting system in *jingju* has changed a great deal during the last forty years, the function of a text remains the same. Many of the plays in written form today are in fact records of an actual performance in the old days when "oral instructions and heart-to-heart teaching" between the master and his apprentice were the common practice. There are many plays in this category that do not even have a story, and a "play" becomes a "frame" in which the unique skills of the actor are displayed. In the early 1920s, Mei Lanfang, Cheng Yanqiu and other *jingju* reformers began to invite writers to write plays or to reorganize the traditional repertoire for their troupes. In such circumstances, the writers were quite conscious of whom they were writing for, and aware of which of the four skills the actors were good at. Their scripts gave stars ample opportunity to demonstrate their talents. Since the late 1950s when the Government encouraged the development of a new repertoire, more and more emphasis has been laid on playwriting. However, before putting the pen to paper, a playwright needs to think about the performers first, because, in *jingju*, the performers' skills dominate the stage, and the number one priority for a written script is to leave enough space for performers who will then be able to make their own creations and to display their vocal and physical genius.

Conventionalization: the Soul of Jingju

Old masters always tell their apprentices: "You must show the audience your own unique skills." This is both a demand from *jingju* as a genre to the actor, and also an expectation of the audience. Although all the stage techniques are guided by the conventionalization, they are the tangible embodiment of this aesthetic concept. Conventionalization therefore determines the distinct processes of training an actor, making a good actor and creating a role in a new play.

Training starts from about twelve years old and the training usually takes about seven years.[17] After the founding of People's Republic of China in 1949, several state-run *jingju* schools were established where students could learn *jingju* as a vocation. They have general classes too, including Chinese, history and mathematics (some now have English classes as well). Students are assigned to specific role types (although it is also possible to expect a talented actor to acquire the skills of a few sub-type character roles) as soon as they are enrolled, but have to go through various general physical and vocal exercises. They also have specific one-to-one training. The ideal of an actor is to master the four skills of singing, reciting, acting and dance (martial arts), but each individual can be a specialist in one or two particular areas.[18] Training is rigorous and can be tedious, because each stylized gesture or body movement has its own inflexible rules, and the height, the width or span of any gesture/movement has to be accurate.[19] Timing is also crucial, because, for instance, in a martial scene, performers need extremely well-organized cooperation. One person's careless mistake can cause an accident. A good actor devotes his or her whole life to practising for perfection. Apart from basic vocal and physical training, the curriculum is based on the traditional repertoire. Students are taught singing and reciting skills line by line, and proceed from learning simple gesture one by one to more complicated body movements in order to master acting techniques. Thus after about four to five years' training, young students can perform a number of plays from the traditional repertoire. These performances are normally a reproduction of tutor's teaching. A teenager cannot be expected to understand a royal concubine's disappointment, embarrassment and despair when she plays Concubine Yang in the famous repertoire piece *The Drunken Beauty* (*Gui fei zui jiu*).[20] However, if she can reproduce even a part of what she has learned, vocally and physically, she will be able to convey the feelings described above to a certain degree even though she has no personal understanding of them.[21]

The secret of the young girl's performance again lies in the concept of conventionalization. All conventional gestures or movements, even facial expressions on the stage, are formed on the basis of the understanding of the roles in certain situations at a particular moment in the story. They have been first created and then varied by generations of actors who have played the same role in the same play. Thus, these established patterns or sets have not only a physical content, but also a real emotional significance. This feature makes it feasible, for instance, for a child actor to play the part of a sixty-year old and the audience will have no difficulty in accepting this. On the other hand, this feature also serves as the criterion to distinguish an excellent actor from a group of ordinary ones. Li Yuru, a celebrated *jingju* actress, wrote to the authors of this article: "Conventionalization shows the difference between an artist and an artisan. An artisan only demonstrates techniques, while an artist transforms techniques into flesh and blood."[22]

No doubt, techniques are an essential aspect of the performance art of *jingju*, and they are essential for making an actor. Nonetheless, they are merely tools and are used to present actions and to reveal the inside feelings and the characterization of the roles (Li Yuru, 25 October 1998). In other words, only when the actor understands the meaning of conventions, do the gestures and movements come alive. Let us take *The Drunken Beauty* as an example. Many great masters have performed this play and each had their own style of presenting it. However, the Mei (Lanfang) school now dominates the play, and therefore most actresses follow his style. In this traditional repertoire, there is a body movement called *wo yu*, literally meaning "reclining fish". It calls for considerable strength of legs and the back as well as a good control of both. First, the performer stands with the feet in the position that a Western woman adopts when curtseying, then slowly squats down on the heels. While still in the squatting position, the back and the head of the performer are brought even lower until they touch the floor, with the face turns upwards. The slower the action, the more difficult it is and of course the more skill it demands. Conventionally, *wo yu* appeared three times in the play. Mei Lanfang copied the movement from his master when he was a young apprentice. But the more he did it, the more he was bothered by the questions: "What does this mean and why should the concubine do it?"[23] He finally solved the puzzle by using this movement in order to smell flowers. The concubine then picks a flower and puts it in her hair. She suddenly remembers that the Emperor is not present and she becomes angry again. Mei also reduced the body movements to two to avoid repetition. Thus *wo yu* and "smelling flowers" were linked and became conventions and rules for this play. Now comes the question of what Mei's disciples should do. Should they merely follow him or can they further develop the conventions that Mei established after he broke with the old law? This is actually a question beyond one concrete play, because any genre with a rich tradition faces the dilemma of making progress as well as keeping the conventions.

Li Yuru's own experience of performing *The Drunken Beauty* seems to offer us some insights into this old riddle. She learned different styles of *The Drunken Beauty* from Mei and other masters, and performed this play hundreds of times since she was nine. As every apprentice does, she first imitated, but then tried to blend the differing styles she had learned and to incorporate her own creative ideas into the role. Talking about *wo yu*, Li explained:

> I changed the two *wo yu* back into three, because I wanted to show the Royal Concubine's different moods and the process by which she gets more and more drunk. After taking off her outside gown, she comes on the stage again, rather tipsy. Suddenly she finds a pot of flowers on the ground, which have been brought out by the two eunuchs. She bends down to smell the flowers , the first *wo yu* [see Figure 2]. These flowers are appreciated by her, but she herself, more attractive than these flowers, is simply abandoned! She becomes annoyed by the flowers and moves brusquely away the first pot. Then she catches sight of the second pot. This is a golden crab-apple. It has so many blossoms on it. She crouches

down to sniff at the flowers one after another (second *wo yu*). They are beautiful but who else can be bothered to look at them? She feels such empathy with the flowers that she does not want to look at them any more. She is dizzy and finds it difficult to stand up. However, at this moment, she glances at the third pot. It is a peony. The flowers are huge and striking. She almost throws herself at them. This time I make a few turns before I do the fairly quick third *wo yu* to demonstrate the drunk concubine's uncontrolled body and unbalanced manner, and then use a few gestures of the water-sleeves to show her failed attempt to pick the flower. She is drunk, she cannot focus. She is carried away by the beauty of the flowers and almost forgets her own situation. She picks a flower, and puts it in her hair. She stands up slowly and gracefully to show the pretty flower and prettier self to the Emperor. However what faces her is the empty chair. She becomes frustrated, throws the flower on the ground and finally gives vent to her anger by stamping on it.

In this vivid description Li not only tells us how conventions evolve and develop, but also shows us how an actor in *jingju* creates a role. First of all, her design of the series of turns, movements of water-sleeve, the slow motion of standing up and moving around as well as the steps, was based on her awareness of what a drunk person in everyday life does. Secondly, the drunk person's lack of body control has to be expressed by the fully controlled body of the actress. Various conventional gestures and movements are limited by the basic patterns, music and percussion, but according to the actress's understanding of the character as well as the plot, new series of the basic units can be created. And therefore thirdly, the process of creating a role is based on the conventions the actor masters. The more an actor can do, the more transformations and variations s/he can make.[24]

Furthermore, Li's narration of her own performance also points to the mental status of an actor on the stage. *Jingju* performers must be good at monitoring their mastering of the four skills as well as assessing the performing space to see if it is safe enough to do any acrobatics. They can never afford to lose control of their bodies or emotions (for instance, a real fit of weeping would cause loss of voice and destroy the heavy make-up). It is notable that Li always uses the third person when she refers to the role, and she never forgets with what body movements/gestures she can employ to

Figure 2. Royal Concubine Yang, performed by Li Yuru, smells flowers in the wo yu (reclining fish) scene from The Drunken Beauty. Photo courtesy of Li Yuru.

present the role. Thus, for a *jingju* actor on the stage there is no "process of conversion to the role" like the one actors in realistic theatre are expected to undertake. The following theatre proverb illustrates the relationship between an actor and a role: "[If you] pretend to be a dragon, [you should] look like a dragon; to be a tiger, then look like a tiger". The first task (to pretend) involves all the types of techniques that have been discussed, while the second (to look like) stresses the actor's awareness of being watched.

Since the theatre experience must be shared by both performers and audiences, Chinese spectators are in a similarly demanding situation to that of the performers, because they have to imagine and fully participate in the action on the stage. *Jingju* audiences can never be passive observers who look through the transparent "fourth wall". They are not supplied with any illusion; on the contrary, they have to work hard with the performers to create the imagination in order to make the theatrical activity. In the *wo yu* scene in *The Drunken Beauty*, the pots of flowers are in the mind's eye for both the performer and the spectators. None of the theatrical tricks Li Yuru explained above would work without the audience's cooperation.

Meanwhile the aesthetic psychology of the *jingju* spectators is similar to the experience of those appreciating an opera or a ballet. *Jingju* audiences often go to the same play again and again for the sake of appreciating the unique skills of different performers, and sometimes merely to see one particular star who often has his/her own group of fans. Audiences usually know the plot and arias by heart, and often hum or even sing along with the performers. The theatre proverb quoted earlier in fact also throws light on the expectations of the audience: they come to see how an actor with various unique skills pretends to be a "dragon", and to judge whether or not the actor really looks like a "dragon". They applaud success and boo those performers whom they do not like. Such audience reactions can be traced back to the Ming dynasty (1368-1644).[25]

In addition, *jingju* spectators not only need to be properly motivated to join in the theatrical process, they also have to acquire the knowledge of conventions on which the tacit mutual understanding between the actor and the audience is based. When a *jingju* troupe tours abroad, most audiences are fascinated by their acrobatic skills as well as their colourful costumes and striking make-up. As regards the acting, even with the sub-titles, they tend to find it "opaque".[26] Unfortunately, more and more young audiences in China today have the same problems. They do not like *jingju* for many reasons, but one of them is that they are not familiar with conventions, and *jingju* becomes opaque for them too. In order to win back audiences and subsequently rescue the genre, the Shanghai *Jingju* Troupe has, since the 1980s, given seminars and performances in schools and universities. They also help students to organize amateur *jingju* clubs. Quite a few *jingju* troupes in other big cities have followed suit. In the course of an experiment at Beijing University in 1990, most students, who had never seen a *jingju* production before were asked to see *The Drunken Beauty* and then given a seminar on *jingju*, found the genre interesting, and some of them wanted to see other productions.[27] This demonstrates firstly, that audiences must be active rather than passive observers in the theatrical experience in *jingju*; secondly, if *jingju* wants to stop its popularity from declining, it needs not only to enhance its conventions but also, perhaps more importantly, to train its audiences. *Jingju* education, pioneered by the Shanghai *Jingju* Troupe, is a significant step forward in the development of the form at the turn of the century.

Li Yuru stated in her letter that "Conventionalization is the soul of *jingju*". As the aesthetic principle for the theatrical form, it shares the attributes of Chinese philosophy that emphasizes the dialectic aspects and their constant movement in everything. For example, *yin* and *yang* are typical patterns of this process, in which the two contradictory elements move, change and exchange places frequently and permanently. More importantly, as the *yin-yang* diagram shows, only when the two integrate with each other, does the whole exist. The concept of conventionalization is formed in the same way – techniques and art serve to complement each other. This brings both advantages and disadvantages to the stage. Requiring maintenance of the conventional patterns and rules, it also demands innovative creations. The discussion of the *wo yu* episode in *The Drunken Beauty* shows us that without such techniques the art cannot exist. However, without art, techniques are worthless. Art in this context does not mean the superficial beauty of gestures or body movements, but pin-points the substance of the concept.

A brief summary of the origin of the concept may help us to gain a more profound understanding of the idea of conventionalization. The formulation of the various conventions was in fact the result of the limited physical conditions of the theatre. Small troupes toured around the country, and therefore costumes had to be general in order to be used for any historical period. There was no lighting or scenery, and performers had to be skilful enough to represent time and place. Due to the open and flexible performing space, all the actions on the stage had to be exaggerated, and thus body movements and gestures, which were originally taken from everyday life gradually turned into dances while words became songs. Each generation of actors makes their own contributions; conventions enrich and expand, and conventionalization has become the guiding principle for *jingju*.

With the passing of time, form unfortunately often tends to take priority over content. Zhang Yunxi, a famous martial *sheng* and an important figure in *jingju* education, sadly noted that many performers today do not even know what the actions they perform mean or how the stage techniques are related to the play. He concluded that if this continues, conventionalization will eventually lose its vitality.[28] Techniques are important in *jingju*, and provide actors with what Barba calls 'absolute advice', however many performers are so overwhelmed by the unique skills that they neglect the play itself. Adding unnecessary martial arts to cater for the audience's taste or repeating the same movement or lingering on a high note until an audience begins to clap are all typical by-products of conventionalization. Due to rigid patterns and limitations, some practitioners simply imitate and become mechanical artisans.

No doubt, each younger generation faces more difficult tasks, especially if they want to perform the traditional repertoire, for all the conventions in these plays have been set, further developed and delicately polished by their predecessors, and they seem to be perfect already.[29] How will Li Yuru's disciples and other younger actresses who perform *The Drunken Beauty* create new roles for themselves? This is certainly not an easy question to answer and will be more difficult in practice. However, the general consensus is that if *jingju* wants not only to survive but also to flourish, conventions will have to be reformed and to develop. Many *jingju* masters pointed to the fact that the strength of *jingju* lies in its constant innovations. [30] Numerous examples can be found in its history showing that masters were in fact great reformers. Mei Lanfang's introduction of the *erhu*, a string instrument, to the musical accompaniment, changes in make-up, a new role type of *huashan* (a blending of *qingyi* and *huadan*, which was based on the creation of his teacher Wang Yaoqin), Cheng Yanqiu's new style of melodies as well as the water-sleeve movements, and Zhou Xinfang's use of the beard and steps are all good examples. Some famous schools of singing and acting disappeared simply because the successors attempted to keep the traditions without making any reforms in them. It is certain that exclusively formalized or rigidly stable conventionalization can only lead the genre to a dead end. The life-long task of *jingju* practitioners is in fact to seek the balance between tradition and creativity.

Notes

1   There are different terms for this theatrical form: *jingju* (Beijing drama) and *jingxi* (Beijing theatre) are used on the mainland, *guoju* (the national drama) was once used on the mainland but has vanished since 1949, yet is still used in Taiwan. In Taiwan it is also referred to as *pingju*, because Beijing was called Beiping during the period when the central government of the Republic was based in Nanjing. It is also interesting to note that the character jing in Chinese also means "capital".

2   There are two main types of theatre in China. One is spoken drama (*huaju*), the modern theatre, which did not emerge until the beginning of this century, and is derived from an imitation of Western theatre at the turn of the nineteenth and twentieth centuries. The other is the traditional theatre, which is called xiqu in Chinese. The term is often translated into English as operas, and its literal meaning is "theatrical melodies". These two types of theatre retain quite different characteristics.

3   This is the local theatre in the present-day Shaanxi province, in north-western China. "Qin" was the old name of this area.

4   Both terms are referred to in the regional theatre of the south-eastern area of Jiangsu province today.

5   Zhao Taimou, 'The National Theatre (*Guoju*)' in Yu Shangyuan (ed), *The National Drama Movement* (Guoju yundong) Series of Chinese Drama and Theatre, 1st edition, September 1927, p. 14. All translations from Chinese into English are by the authors unless otherwise indicated.

6   Wang Guowei, *Wang Guowei, Criticism on Traditional Chinese Drama and Theatre* (Wang Guowei xiqu lunwen ji), 1st edition (Beijing: Zhongguo Xiji Chubanshe, 1984), p. 161.

7   Mei Lanfang, 'The Performance Art of Jingju (*Zhongguo jingju de biaoyan yishu*)' in Chinese Dramatists Association (ed), *Selected Works of Mei Lanfang* (Mei Lanfang wenji), 1st edition 2nd printing (Beijing: Zhongguo Xiju Chubanshe, 1981), pp. 31-32.

8   Chinese authorities use different divisions of sub-types in roles. This article adopts the system used by Mei Lanfang in his paper "The Performance Art of *Jingju*", pp. 14-40.

9   All the founders of the five female schools are male actors.

10   Liu Zengfu, the author of *Jingju Painted face: Patterns and Commentary*, collected 424 painted face patterns, but in the book listed 264 coloured ones as the most commonly used in *jingju*.

11 We should not forget that, in any artistic form, there are always exceptions. This applies to the painted face. For instance, the famous character of Judge Pao (*Bao Gong* in Chinese) in the *jing* role is a man full of intelligence, wisdom, courage, resourcefulness.

12 In *jingju* there is a proverb concerning the costumes: "Better to wear the worn costumes rather than the new ones which are wrong." This proverb indicates first of all, the importance of the costumes in this genre. Secondly, the meaning of "wrong" here is not wrong in the sense of the given circumstance of the particular story, but "wrong" according to the strict rules.

13 Xi Shi, 'About the Water-sleeves (*Wian hua shuixiu*)' in *People's Daily* [international edition] (Renmin ribao), 30 January 1991, p. 8.

14 Mei Lanfang, *op. cit.,* p. 132.

15 Chen Youhan, *Exploration of the Aesthetics of Chinese Performance Art* (Xiqu biaoyan meixue tansuo) 1st edition (Beijing: Zhongguo Xiji Chubanshe, 1985), p. 184.

16 This used to be an episode from a long play *The Famen Temple* (*Famen si*), but it is now performed on its own. There is a large traditional repertoire in *jingju* of independent short plays, which were originally highlights taken from longer plays.

17 After 1949, *jingju* schools were taken into the secondary education system, and therefore candidates have first to complete a primary school course and become *jingju* students when about twelve or thirteen. They are older than the apprentices were formerly.

18 Some students, especially boys whose voice does not recover from breaking at their adolescence, will then be trained for martial arts, or as the players of musical instruments. They can also be trained to become specialists for make-up or costumes, including props.

19 A typical day for *jingju* students starts at about six in the morning. They begin with basic training (similar to bar work for a ballet dancer) supervised by the tutor(s) including stretching the limbs and the back, kicking the legs, different walking steps, and other acrobatic exercises or martial arts. Junior and senior students are assigned different tasks. After the morning physical training, students go through various vocal exercises. Afternoons are spent either on general subjects or in smaller groups to learn a specific role from a tutor. Upper years have rehearsals. Junior students are expected to play walk-on parts in the performances given by the senior students. The morning basic training is carried out by all the professionals throughout their lives.

20 This play is older than *jingju* itself, and it originated from the Han melody (*handiao*) and Hui Theatre (*huiju*), the two predecessors of the genre. The title of the present play has different English translations: *Concubine Becomes Intoxicated* by Jo Riley, *The Drunken Concubine* by Elizabeth Halson, and *Drunken Beauty* by C. Scott.

It is about the famous Royal Concubine Yang of the Tang Dynasty. Having received the imperial order from the Emperor to have a dinner with him, Yang leaves her own chamber to go to the garden in a joyful mood. But when she arrives, she is informed by the eunuchs that the Emperor has gone to see his other concubine. Yang first is embarrassed, then becomes disappointed and frustrated. She starts drinking by herself and finally gets very drunk and sadly goes back to her own quarters. The plot is so simple that the fifty minutes of performance are dedicated to the roles' songs and dances rather than telling a story.

21 This characteristic of *jingju* acting was once noticed by Brecht, and used to support his argument of A-effect. After talking about Mei Lanfang's demonstration at a reception party, Brecht went on:

To the westerner what matters is that his actions should be unconscious; otherwise they would be degraded. By comparison with Asiatic acting our own art still seems hopelessly parsonical ...

For the actor it is difficult and taxing to conjure up particular inner moods or emotions night after night; it is simpler to exhibit the outer signs which accompany these emotions and identify them. In this case, however, there is not the same automatic transfer of emotions to the spectator, the same emotional infection. The alienation effect intervenes, not in the form of absence of emotion, but in the form of emotions which need not correspond to those of the character portrayed.

See Bertolt Brecht, *Brecht on Theatre: The Development of An Aesthetic,* translated by John Willett (London: Eyre Methuen, 1973), p. 94.

22 Li Yuru is the mother of Ruru Li. All quotations used in this article are from two letters (25 & 29 October 1998) to the authors in reply to various questions about her experiences on the *jingju* stage.

At the time of writing, Li Yuru was seventy-five years old and a *jingju* actress since she was nine. She was elected by "Forum Daily" (*Liyan bao*) in 1937 as one of "the four Jades", the four nationally renowned young *jingju* actresses who all have the character for "jade" in their names. Li studied three different *dan* schools and was lucky to have the founding masters to teach her. She toured in Europe, the former USSR, and other East European and Asian countries. Her last appearance on the stage was when she was sixty-eight. She is still the artistic advisor for Shanghai *Jingju* Troupe, and teaches students occasionally.

23 Mei Lanfang, *A Forty-year Life on the Stage* (Wutai shengghu sishinian), recorded by Xu Jichuan (Beijing: Zhongguo Xiju Chubanshe, 1980), p. 30.

24 In old days, if an actor wanted to join a *jingju* troupe, the owner (usually the leading actor) always asked one question: "How many plays have you learned to perform?" This question indicates the truth that in the performance art of *jingju* the more plays an actor has learned the more patterns or conventions s/he has mastered, and therefore it will be easier for the actor to create a new role in new plays.

25 Zhang Dai, a scholar in the Ming dynasty (1368-1644), vividly described how knowledgeable and involved the audience was during a performance: "No sooner had an actor forgotten a word than someone in the audience would shout the correction. The crowd hooted in derision, and the play would have to start again". See Lu Erting, *A Draft History in* Kunju *Performance* (Kunju yanchu shi gao), (Shanghai: Wenyi Chubanshe, 1980), p. 175.

26 See John Gillies, 'Chinese Performance/ Western Perspective' in *Proceedings of the International Conference, Shakespeare in China: Perspectives and Performances* (Shanghai, September 1998).

27 Luo Zheng, *Seminars on* Jingju *for University Students* (Dazhuanyuanxiao jingju jiangzuo), (Shanghai: Wenyi Chubanshe, 1980), p. 27.

28 Zhang Yunxi, 'The Actor Must Understand the Meaning and Attribute of Conventions (*Yanyuan yao mingliao chenshi dongzuo de shuxing yu hanyi)*' in *Chinese Drama and Theatre* (Zhongguo xiju) (Beijing, 1991), pp. 58-59.

29 Jo Riley correctly points out that in Chinese theatre each actor does not stand alone on the stage as an individual representing a role. Rather, s/he is overshadowed by the inheritance of his/her teachers and the traditions of the particular genre. See Riley, *Chinese Theatre and the Actor in Performance* (Cambridge: CUP, 1997).

30 Xu Lanyuan, 'Our Predecessors' Innovations (*Tantan qianbei yiren de ge jiu chuangxin)*' in *Reference to Theatrical Art Vol. 5* (Xiiju yishu cankao ziliao 5), Chinese Dramatists Association, Anhui Branch (Hefei, 1963), p. 72.

7 "Your Mother is Up Here Working!"

Bette Midler, the Continental Baths, and the Mainstreaming of Gay Male Sensibility

Kevin Winkler

"Look alive! Your mother is up here working!" the diva commands. It could be Madonna silencing a multi-ethnic mix of concertgoers at Madison Square Garden. Or RuPaul admonishing the studio audience for his prime time VH1 variety show. Or Roseanne quieting a raucous comedy club crowd. It is, in fact, Bette Midler humorously acknowledging her den mother status to an adoring cluster of towel-clad gay men at New York City's subterranean Continental Baths more than twenty-five years ago. That a quintessential gay slang expression (traditionally reserved for that personage – usually a drag queen – deserving of the utmost respect and deference)[1] has travelled so thoroughly from the margins of gay camp humour to the mainstream lexicon is merely one example of the influence of the performing ethos Bette Midler developed in front of her early gay men-only audience. Those few square feet of space she and her audience occupied at the Continental were the site of a head-on collision between the post-Stonewall gay liberation movement and the whole of contemporary show business. The Stonewall riots, sexual experimentation, gay rights, Fire Island, and the drag queen subculture all crashed into Carmen Miranda, Sophie Tucker, Janis Joplin, Judy Garland, and the Andrews Sisters. And when the wreckage was cleared, an artist emerged who, as cultural critic Michael Bronski has noted, "brought some of the pleasure and the freedom that gay talk, life, and camp have always promoted to mainstream audiences. She has been a major conductor of gay sensibility to the straight world".[2] For the purposes of this chapter, I define that gay sensibility as a white urban male homosexual outlook and world-view circa the 1970s which exhibited itself most uninhibitedly in the self-segregated world of the bathhouse.

Bette Midler was a largely unknown singer-actress when she first stepped into an open space near the swimming pool of the Continental Bath and Health Club to sing for its patrons. After failing to generate much enthusiasm in her initial appearances as a traditional chanteuse, she reconceived her performances to play specifically to the sexuality of her audiences and, in so doing, adapted many of the characteristics of gay male culture to her own persona. Midler's act created a sensation and, through her performances at the Continental over a two-year period, established both her reputation as a singer and comedienne, and that of the Continental as a legitimate and influential performance venue.

Bathhouses as sites for sexual activity for gay men have been part of the social landscape of gay New York since the early days of the twentieth century.[3] Historian

George Chauncey notes that beyond providing safe, private accommodation for sexual encounters, "the baths were also important social centers, where gay men could meet openly, discuss their lives, and build a circle of friends. Their distinctive character fostered a sense of community among their patrons".[4] As important as they were to New York's gay male community, by the 1960s the "tubs", as they were called in gay slang, were dank, filthy places whose squalid conditions were a clear indication of the contempt in which their homosexual patrons were held by the predominantly heterosexual owners. Stephen Ostrow, a married, openly bisexual entrepreneur and bathhouse patron, felt that an establishment offering clean, well-maintained facilities and respectful treatment could dominate this small but lucrative niche market.[5] When his Continental Bath and Health Club opened in September 1968 it was New York City's largest gay bathhouse, boasting unheard-of amenities, including an Olympic-size swimming pool, weight-training facilities, deluxe bedroom suites, film screenings, and nightly buffets.[6] Ostrow sought to create a full-scale resort for gay men, with live entertainment an integral part of its attractions. The Continental's first talent booking, a husband-and-wife folk-singing duo, played weekends for three uneventful months in early 1970. Scouting for a follow-up act, a young singer and actress was recommended to Ostrow, who signed her for eight weekends at the Continental beginning in July.

By 1970, Bette Midler had been in New York City for five years, and her professional resume was a hodgepodge of Broadway musicals, downtown avant-garde performance, and low- (or non-) paying cabaret singing engagements. Significantly, Midler's arrival in New York coincided with a burgeoning Off-off-Broadway scene, much of which was marked by gay camp humour, satire, and parody. Two key figures in this movement made strong impressions on her and likely influenced the development of her performances at the Continental Baths. Midler became part of a very loosely-based repertory company for playwright Tom Eyen, performing at Cafe LaMama in the title role of his *Miss Nefertiti Regrets*, a campy musical spoof of the Egyptian queen. She was also a frequent attendee at Charles Ludlam's Ridiculous Theatrical Company and later acknowledged their impact on her.[7]

On the eve of her first performance at the Continental, a friend of Midler's visited the bathhouse and saw an announcement of her upcoming appearance. He immediately phoned to tell her that a drag queen was appearing at the Continental using her name.[8] Midler roared with laughter and used the line during her first performance. It probably earned her her sole laugh that night, as the audience of twenty or thirty men sitting near the pool offered only tepid response to her torch songs and period ballads. Midler quickly recognized that the standards and conventions of other nightclubs and cabarets did not apply at the Continental. The space was noisy and unfocused, requiring a performer to fight for the audience's attention. More to the point was her realization that many of the men in the audience were weekend regulars who expected a different show each night, and that entertainment was subsidiary to the baths' primary purpose, as she later bluntly acknowledged when explaining how her performances evolved at the Continental: "The audience there wouldn't settle for half-ass. If I'd kept my distance, they'd have lost interest because there were too many other things going on in the building that were more fun".[9]

The conventional dividing line between onstage and offstage was blurred at the Continental. The fact that the audience was towel-clad and standing or sitting casually on the floor added to the intimacy of the performer-audience interaction. No stage or platform was set up; instead, the performer appropriated a portion of the floor adjacent to the swimming pool to create a modest performance space where, a few minutes earlier, none had existed. The backstage dressing room was a corner of Ostrow's office situated up a short flight of stairs. After dressing, the performer was required to descend the stairs, pass the open bathroom and shower area, and interact with the semi-nude (or possibly nude) patrons before arriving "onstage". This encroachment of offstage space onto onstage space was such that the performer was "on" the second she left the dressing room, playing to everyone in the Continental's basement well before she entered the designated performance space and faced her audience proper.

This unorthodox performance arena required a radically different approach and energy, but also offered Midler unexpected opportunities. By the end of a month Midler's act was nearly unrecognizable from her first appearance, and in those alterations she laid the foundation for the rest of her career. Key to these changes was her appropriation of gay camp elements into every facet of her performance. While Susan Sontag, in her foundational essay, 'Notes on Camp', acknowledges the strong connection between homosexuality and an appreciation of camp,[10] in recent years others have claimed camp as central to gay male sensibility.[11] Writer Jack Babuscio describes this sensibility as "a heightened awareness of certain human complications of feeling that spring from the fact of social oppression".[12] Camp, then, is "those elements in a person, situation, or activity that express, or are created by, a gay sensibility".[13] The gay camp elements incorporated by Midler included humour, visual presentation, and song selection.

In developing her style and persona at the Continental, Midler was aided immeasurably by a number of gay male collaborators, and she would continue to depend on the talents and sensibilities of gay men as her career thrived.[14] Crucially, her friend Bill Hennessey urged her to let "the insanity, the zaniness of her humour ... come out both in her patter between songs and in her whole attitude and awareness of her image onstage".[15] Hennessy began creating jokes, gags, and characters for Midler to talk about in her act, and was instrumental in helping Midler exploit the mutual identification between herself and her audience. The Jewish girl from Hawaii who left home seeking success in the theatre had much in common with the men who regularly came to the baths seeking sex and a sense of community. They shared an outsider, or misfit, status reinforced by the clandestine nature of the venue: Midler performed unadvertised late-night performances for a small, "select" group in an establishment that was still considered disreputable by most people.

Babuscio describes gay camp humour as "a means of dealing with a hostile environment and, in the process, of defining a positive identity".[16] Midler found her perfect embodiment of this humour in a newly-created alter-ego, "The Divine Miss M.", who proved to be the catalyst she needed to connect intimately with these men, as she later recalled.

> At the Continental Baths I was playing to people who are always on the outside looking
> in.... And so I created the character of The Divine Miss M. She's just a fantasy, but she's
> useful at showing people what that outsider's perspective is.[17]

Richard Dyer has linked the value of camp to its use in deflating the power and
"mystique" of masculinity.[18] As "The Divine Miss M.", she joked about sex the same way
gay men did: puncturing (straight) male pretensions and reveling in outrageousness.
"Miss M." would frequently speak in an exaggerated, drag-queen manner, cajoling, or
"dishing" her audience good-naturedly. She established an intimate dialogue with her
audience by talking to them in their own jargon about issues other straight performers
claimed ignorance of. She joked about Fire Island ("health spa for hairdressers")[19], their
mating habits at the baths ("Even Josephine the Plumber couldn't get the stains out of
these sinks"), and her own status as a sort of den mother to them ("Oh God! Why can't I
be like other girls?"). She spoke in the knowing, insider manner gay men often do about
show business figures ("Martha Raye was beaten up by the Viet Cong in the Christopher
Street tearoom"). She adopted gay slang expressions, referring to the Continental as "the
pits", and joking about the attire of her audience as "tacky". She referred to herself and
to anything deserving the highest form of praise as "divine", and soon elevated that
expression to gay cult status. She minced and sashayed around the stage, sometimes
verging on caricature to become, as Bronski put it, "a female female impersonator".[20]
Midler acknowledged and made fun of this drag queen element of her presentation. For
instance, an advertisement for her final performance at the Continental in 1972 features
images of the star as Carmen Miranda and Barbra Streisand, two perennial female
impersonator favorites. When performing "Marijuana", a melodramatic tale of a
woman's enslavement to the drug, Midler approximated the styles and gestures of both
women for comic effect. She wore a towel and plastic fruit on her head in a ludicrous
recreation of an exotic Miranda headdress, while assuming the preening gestures of
Streisand at her most dramatic.

Yet Midler exuded a strong female sexuality, revelling in her body, and as much
concerned with sexual liberation as her audience. She was unquestionably a heterosexual
woman with strong appetites, but her appraisals of the physical attributes of men were
directed to an audience of peers. While her humour (which became an increasingly
important part of her performances) could be abrasive, Midler tempered it with a
genuinely warm personality and self-deprecating wit. In short, as James Spada writes,
"She was the first non-gay, non-drag queen performer ever to relate to these men in this
way".[21]

The camp element of her act took visual form as Midler combined fashions from a
dizzying variety of eras, all of which, by contemporary standards, appeared gauche and
impossibly dated. Andrew Ross has written of the "camp effect" achieved when
"products" of an earlier era that have lost their currency are reclaimed and given a
contemporary reinterpretation.[22] Midler's fashion "products", including Merry Widow
corsets, halter tops with no bra, wraparound skirts slit to the thigh, and skintight lamé
pants all contributed to her new "trash with flash" look. Spring-o-later shoes (a type of
platform shoe that sat dangerously atop an extra-long, narrow heel) facilitated her

mincing walk. She stopped straightening her curly hair and instead let it provide a frizzy frame to her face, which added to the animation of her features. Midler's "trash with flash" look was a form of drag or transvestitism whose effect differed significantly from that achieved by female impersonators. Whereas female impersonation seeks to create the illusion of femaleness while camouflaging the male impersonator's real sex, Midler's drag boldly emphasized her own physical attributes, particularly a full, lush bosom, and made her appear a more vibrant and sexualized woman. The sexually-charged setting and the fact that the audience was semi-nude encouraged Midler to be more explicit in presenting her own sexuality, and she would fiercely shake or sensuously caress her braless breasts, depending on the song she was singing. She frequently took her final bow in a towel like those worn by the audience, and offered a flash of her buttocks.

In both costume and gesticulation, her performance embodied what Babuscio calls the subversiveness of camp: "A means of illustrating those cultural ambiguities and contradictions that oppress us all, gay and straight, and in particular women".[23] By flaunting "trashy" clothes and using vulgar gestures not used by female singers in more traditional nightclub settings, Midler subverted the notion of "passing for straight" (e.g. conforming to conventional feminine standards of decorum) and further underlined the outsider status she shared with her audience.

Midler's song selection further accommodated a gay camp sensibility. Babuscio points out that "while camp advocates the dissolution of hard and inflexible moral rules, it pleads, too, for a morality of sympathy".[24] This "morality of sympathy" was present in Midler's mining of trash pop culture to explore the value in forgotten rock and roll, girl group jingles, 1940s swing, and cheesy pop songs. Her act became a panorama of American popular music, but rather than a mishmash of different styles and eras, the songs were unified by her sense of purpose as a singing actress. Kurt Weill, the Dixie Cups, Bob Dylan, and Glenn Miller were all treated with equal respect in her interpretations. Midler's embrace of songs and musical genres that other singers found of dubious quality demonstrated her "morality of sympathy" for outsiders and underdogs, and connected strongly with the men at the Baths.

As word spread that an exciting new entertainer had been discovered at the Continental, the comparison of Bette Midler with Judy Garland and Barbra Streisand was a recurring theme.[25] Gay men clearly identified with the intensely emotional style, unorthodox beauty, and off-centre humour of all three, but there were crucial differences in the women's means of communicating with that audience. Garland and Streisand can be seen as products of the pre-Stonewall era in that both observed a heterosexual hegemony in their performances. That is, an unspoken contract existed between Garland and Streisand and their gay male audience which acknowledged that their performances were heterosexual presentations. When Garland sang "The Man That Got Away", or Streisand performed "People", for instance, the songs were clearly intended to describe male-female love, and gay men were required to filter their identification with these women through this prism of heterosexual presentation.

Midler, on the other hand, through her appearances at the Continental, established herself as a product of the post-Stonewall gay liberation era. It would have been unthinkable for Garland in the 1950s and 60s to explicitly acknowledge and play to her large gay fan base, and Streisand, who was championed early on by gay men who made up the audience at Greenwich Village clubs like the Lion and the Bon Soir, ignored that audience as she moved quickly into mainstream success. At the Continental there was no ignoring the fact that the entire towel-clad audience was, at least for their time at the bathhouse, gay-identified, and Midler openly embraced them as such. So intense was her identification with this audience, that when she paused to sing a dramatic ballad, the men had no need to filter the sentiments of the song through a heterosexual prism. Midler closed the distance that other straight performers kept from gay audiences, thereby emphasizing her similarities to them.

A prime example of the power of this communication was Midler's interpretation of Bob Dylan's "I Shall Be Released", a rock anthem that in her hands became a fierce declaration of emancipation for women and gay men alike, and was the emotional peak of her performances at the Continental. Starting slowly from a plaintive piano line, Midler's voice gradually grew in strength and anger until, fists clenched and beating the air, she exhorted the audience with the song's refrain, "Any day now". At last, after singing "Any day now, I shall be released," over and over, she climaxed the song by altering the lyrics to sing, "Any day now, *we* shall be released". As the audience spontaneously jumped to its feet and cheered, she bowed deeply from the waist with her arms at her side – an oddly formal gesture used at no other time during the act, but one which reinforced her kinship with them. The unspoken contract of the Garland and Streisand performances did not exist here; instead, a palpable empathy existed between Midler and her gay male audience. It was a moment that resonated with deep emotion.

Midler's acclaim soon moved beyond the gay scene, and Ostrow began allowing women and straight men into the Continental. Midler had now added an original number, "Friends", which would become her theme song. Its bittersweet undercurrent made it a particularly apt number for the bathhouse crowd, who now jockeyed for seats alongside the increasingly straight audiences. On the line, "Here is where I gotta stay", she would squat and slap the floor hard. That one gesture spoke volumes about her relationship with this audience. It acknowledged the debt she owed them while signalling that she would not forget them as her success took her far from the baths.

The most thoughtful writing about Midler at this time examined her unique use of camp. Using Sontag's 'Notes on Camp' as a starting point, *Village Voice* writer Ralph Sepulveda, Jr. noted that whereas Judy Garland in her later appearances became a victim of camp, Midler's knowingness of camp's limitations was her strength. He wrote, "She *understands* camp, knows its sensibility and modes of expression, perceives its links to stereotype notions of homosexual taste".[26] Midler, Sepulveda wrote, remained always in control of camp, using it as a kind of shorthand to connect with the audience; it was this ebullient exploitation of camp that ultimately kept her from *being* camp. Sepulveda was also adamant that Midler's skilful deployment of camp was not only equal to her gifts as a dramatic vocalist, but actually intensified the impact of her serious singing.

Richard Goldstein, in a *New York* magazine feature, recognized that Midler had the ability to bring the kind of vivid, over-the-top performing style beloved by gay men into the rock arena and make it relevant to straight audiences.

Here is the spirit of Tin Pan Alley out there strutting like nobody's business, and the guys in the audience, who have spent a long time sequestering their taste, are seeing the last bastion of true-blue hetero-pop crumble in the face and body and nuance of Bette Midler, who is much more to the point than Alice Cooper, because she's so real-live, so off the wall, and the audience at the Continental loves her and honors her because they know that she is Right.[27]

The excitement created by Midler at the Continental led to a renaissance in the nightclub scene in New York City. New, intimate cabaret rooms and nightclubs began to open all over town, and most borrowed, to varying degrees, from what was perceived as the Continental formula. These clubs offered a more relaxed, informal setting than older, established nightclubs; they encouraged a more personal, revealing approach to material; and they primarily featured female performers with strong appeal to gay men.[28]

"Steve Ostrow's World Famous Continental Baths", as it was newly-christened, was now a legitimate cabaret venue and a high-profile stop on this new cabaret network, known as the "K-Y Circuit", after a lubricant popular among gay men. But soon it was apparent that there would be no other break-out act to follow Bette Midler. An exploitative, heavily-commercial veneer now replaced the Continental's once-palpable feeling of camaraderie and sexual liberation. Ironically, the mainstream success Midler brought to the Continental eventually alienated its core constituency, resulting in its decline both as a performance venue and as a bathhouse.

Despite the Continental's decline, Midler's mainstream success transferred its spirit to a wider audience. Instead of distancing herself from her gay fans, she has essentially elaborated on the template she created at the Baths in every live show and concert tour she has undertaken in the last twenty-five years. Midler recognized in the gay camp style the potential to liberate and broaden the consciousness of everyone, as she once noted to Andy Warhol:

I have that sense of humor. I mean, what they [gay men] think is funny, I think is funny.... Actually everybody has the potential for that humor.... But most people are never exposed to that kind of humor.... They're not told, 'This is funny'. I'm talking about 'camp'. But as soon as they see it, they – change. And they – learn.[29]

"The Divine Miss M." persona played remarkably well with the general public as she has taken on outlandish subjects which, while not specifically gay-identified, have a kind of trash-culture veneer that marked them as "queer." One of her early gambits in translating her Continental humor to straight audiences was to exchange the bathhouse and Fire Island jokes for comic observations on the exotic lingerie of Frederick's of Hollywood. (As a guest on Johnny Carson's final *Tonight Show* broadcast shortly after the South Central Los Angeles riots in 1992, she quipped that her costume was something "I pulled out of Frederick's of Hollywood just before they torched it".[30])

Midler simultaneously celebrated and mocked the conventions of nightclub "lounge acts" by creating two characters, Vicki Eydie, a preening small-time chanteuse, and later, Delores Del Lago, the Toast of Chicago, a singing mermaid who travels by motorized wheelchair. These were essentially drag performances, not so different from her Carmen Miranda caricature at the Continental, as she donned the exaggerated gowns and headdresses of grandstanding, Las Vegas-style performers.

Midler created a popular series of jokes in the style of Sophie Tucker, the bawdy singer and vaudeville star of an earlier generation. "Soph", who told stories mostly concerning her sex life with her perennial boyfriend, Ernie, was a construct similar to The Divine Miss M. Soph talked about men the way straight men often discussed women, appraising their physical attributes and mocking their sexual pretensions. In one of her most widely quoted "Soph" jokes, Ernie criticizes her sexual equipment by telling her she has "no tits and a tight box", to which she witheringly replies, "Ernie, get off my back"![31] Again, Midler expanded her audience by broadening (but not abandoning) the gay camp sensibility of her humour.

Richard Goldstein wrote in 1975 that Midler's most significant contribution was in bringing "the gay show-biz sensibility"[32] to a wide audience, and he praised the gallantry with which she did this: "Bette was the first and finest of gay-style entertainers ... she never denied or deceived her following .... One saw the courage of that alliance and so one's own sensibility was expanded".[33] Indeed, many of the torch, camp, and novelty numbers she first introduced to the men at the Continental are now recognized as standards of American popular music.

Midler's hit recordings, as well as a successful series of film comedies for that most family-oriented movie studio, Walt Disney Pictures, brought Midler's "gay show-biz sensibility" even further into the entertainment mainstream, as Frank Rich noted in 1987:

> The performer one gets in *Ruthless People* [Midler's then-current movie hit] is still identifiable as the Divine Miss M., yet fifteen years later no one finds it necessary to remark on the derivation of her divinity. Her latest fans, indeed, may not even know whence she came.[34]

When she instructs NBC *Today Show* host Katie Couric in the mincing, female impersonator walk she developed on stage at the Continental, Midler's pivotal role in channeling gay sensibility into popular culture becomes abundantly clear.[35]

A star is born: Bette Midler on stage at the Continental Baths (circa. 1972). Photo from The Divine Bette Midler by James Spada (Collier, 1984). No photographer credit.

Her latest fans may be unaware of the origins of the performing style they so eagerly respond to, but Midler has never denied her beginnings. She has consistently paid tribute to the audience that first supported her, noting on one occasion, "I was able to take chances on that stage that I could not have taken anywhere else. Ironically, I was freed from fear by people who, at the time, were ruled by fear. And for that I will always be grateful".[36] Many of the men who counselled and advised her at the outset of her career died of AIDS in the late 1980s, and Midler's performances at countless AIDS benefits and fund-raisers may be seen as a humble and sorrowful salute to the men who first discovered and championed her.[37]

After a decade in Hollywood, where she established herself as a bona fide box office film star, Midler in 1993 returned to the medium that first and most fully revealed her gifts as an artist. The apex of a cross-country tour of her new stage show, *Experience the Divine*, was a record-breaking engagement at Radio City Music Hall which set box-office records. The enormity of the distance Midler had traveled from the depths of the Continental to this venue was conspicuous, as Stephen Holden observed in the *New York Times*:

> What was marginal, gay bathhouse entertainment in the early 1970's is now thoroughly mainstream.... Proclaiming the value of uninhibited self-expression and the freedom to raid the most esoteric corners of pop culture history for whatever is valuable, the genre embodies the urban cultural tone of a liberated era. Ms. Midler reigns as its radiant high priestess.[38]

Stripped of its costumes and production values, her show at this landmark shrine to mass entertainment could easily have been performed for the gay men sitting by the Continental Baths swimming pool. By recalling The Divine Miss M., the show's title forged a link between the audience that first launched her and the adoring crowds of every age, race, and sexual orientation that now greeted her. Mother is still up there working! More than any other performer, Bette Midler took the gay sensibility from the margin to the mainstream, remaining at all times "divine".

Notes

1   Esther Newton, in a note to the reader in *Mother Camp: Female Impersonators in America* (Chicago and London: University of Chicago Press, 1978) refers to the term's use as an "honorific" inferring both affection for, and fear of, older, more accomplished drag performers by younger drag queens and audience members.

2   Michael Bronski, *Culture Clash: The Making of Gay Sensibility* (Boston: South End Press, 1984), p. 108.

3   See 'The Social World of the Baths', pp. 207-225, in George Chauncey's *Gay New York: Gender, Urban Culture, and the Making of the Gay Male World, 1890-1940* (New York: Basic Books, 1994), for a lucid historical overview of New York City bathhouse culture.

4   *ibid.*, p. 224.

5   For biographical information on Ostrow and his creation of the Continental Baths, see Tom Burke, 'King Queen', *Rolling Stone*, 6 May 1976, pp. 36-39, 83-92; John P. LeRoy, 'Le Continental: C'est Moi: An Interview with Steve Ostrow', *Gay*, 18 June 1973, 5, 15; and Perry Deane Young, '"So You're Planning to Spend a

Night at the Tubs?" Here's Some Advice Your Mother Never Gave You', *Rolling Stone*, 15 February 1973, pp. 48-50.

6 See Young; LeRoy, 'Le Continental: C'est Moi'; LeRoy, 'Rub a Dub Dub 3,000 Men in a Tub: New York: Bath Capital of the World', *Gay*, 7 February 1972, 4; and Peter Ogren, 'Doin' the Continental', *Gay*, 6 July 1970, 11 for detailed discussions of the Continental's physical space and amenities.

7 Both James Spada, *The Divine Bette Midler* (New York: Collier, 1984) and Robb Baker, *Bette Midler* (New York: Popular Library, 1975) discuss at some length Midler's early years in New York City, as well as the impact of Eyen's and Ludlam's work on her. Lisa Robinson, 'My Life Story! Bette Midler', *Interview*, October 1972, 16-17, 51 provides Midler's own reminiscences of this period, including her early influences.

8 Dick Leitsch, 'The Whole World's a Bath!', *Gay*, 26 October 1970, p. 16.

9 Charles Michener, 'The Divine Miss M.', *Newsweek*, 22 May 1972, p. 76. The problems Midler faced with the audiences at the Continental are strikingly similar to those encountered by female impersonators at gay nightclubs, as observed by Newton in *Mother Camp*. She writes that "performances for straight audiences can be routinized and unchanged for a year or so because of the constant audience turnover, while in the gay club the stable audience demands changing performances." Newton also notes, "the performer has to battle for the attention of a restless audience for whom the show may be a purely secondary concern." p. 61.

10 Susan Sontag, *Against Interpretation, and Other Essays* (New York: Delta, 1967), pp. 290-291.

11 Vito Russo, 'Camp', *The Advocate*, No. 290, 19 May 1976, pp. 17-18; Richard Dyer, 'It's Being So Camp as Keeps Us Going', *Only Entertainment*, Richard Dyer (London and New York: Routledge, 1992), pp. 135-147; and Andrew Ross, 'Uses of Camp', *Camp Grounds: Style and Homosexuality*, David Bergman, ed. (Amherst: University of Massachusetts Press, 1993), pp. 54-77 are all essential texts for locating the centrality of camp to gay male sensibility.

12 Jack Babuscio, 'Camp and the Gay Sensibility', *Camp Grounds: Style and Homosexuality*, David Bergman, ed. (Amherst: University of Massachusetts Press, 1993), p. 19.

13 *ibid.*, p. 20.

14 Writers Jerry Blatt and Bruce Vilanch proved indispensable collaborators with Midler on comedy material for all her concert tours and live appearances up until Blatt's death in the late 1980s, and Vilanch continues working closely with her to the present. Musical director Marc Shaiman has contributed immeasurably to Midler's musical presentation for several years, writing specialty musical material and guiding her in repertoire. Midler recorded her biggest hit, "Wing Beneath My Wings", at Shaiman's urging.

15 Quoted in Baker, p. 40.

16 Babuscio, p. 27.

17 Charles Michener, 'Here Comes Bette!', *Newsweek*, 17 December 1973, p. 63.

18 Dyer, p. 138.

19 Performance quotes are drawn from a private videotape of a performance by Bette Midler at the Continental Baths, 6 September 1971.

20 Bronski, p. 107.

21 Spada, p. 23.

22 Ross, p. 58.

23 Babuscio, p. 28.

24 Babuscio, p. 21.

25 It is interesting to note that as friends, colleagues, and confidantes, gay men played a crucial part in all three women's development as artists. The bulk of Garland's career at MGM was spent as the front-

ranking star of the Freed unit, the studio's preeminent production unit for musicals, which was heavily populated with gay men. (Jane Feuer's, *The Hollywood Musical* [London: BFI and Bloomington: Indiana University Press, 1993] provides a reading of the gay ethos of the Freed unit's musicals and its impact in defining Garland's image. Christopher Finch, *Rainbow: The Stormy Life of Judy Garland* [New York: Grosset and Dunlap, 1975] and particularly David Shipman, *Judy Garland: The Secret Life of An American Legend* [New York: Hyperion, 1992] provide further discussions of Garland's close working relationships with gay men in the Freed unit, specifically Roger Edens, her musical mentor at MGM, who provided arrangements and specialty material throughout her 14 years at the studio and during her later, concert years.) This working relationship was not unlike Midler's with Bruce Vilanch, who began supplanting the comedy writing of Bill Hennessey soon after her final performances at the Continental in 1972, and who continues working with Midler to this day. Actor-singer Barry Dennen was instrumental in Barbra Streisand's early development as a singer, selecting her song repertoire and coaching her in phrasing and interpretation. (See Barry Dennen, *My Life with Barbra: A Love Story* [Amherst, New York: Prometheus, 1997]). Dennen and Streisand were lovers, similar to Midler's relationship with Ben Gillespie, a dancer who Midler has frequently credited as having introduced her to songs of earlier eras and guiding her stage presentation of that music. Both men later acknowledged their homosexuality. (See Marjorie Rosen, 'Bankable Bette', *Ms*, March 1989, pp. 52-57 and Dennen's book for discussion of this subject.)

26 Ralph Sepulveda, Jr., 'Miss M and the Camp Followers', *Village Voice*, 28 December 1972, p. 30.

27 Richard Goldstein, 'A Night at the Continental Baths', *New York*, 8 January 1973, p. 54.

28 James Gavin's *Intimate Nights: The Golden Age of New York Cabaret* (New York: Grove Weidenfeld, 1991), pp. 297-313, provides a vivid overview of the nightclub scene at the time and Midler's impact on it, both positive and negative.

29 'Andy Warhol Interviews Bette Midler Interviews Andy Warhol', *Interview*, November 1974, p. 6.

30 NBC's "The Tonight Show Starring Johnny Carson", 21 May 1992.

31 HBO's "The Fabulous Bette Midler," 19 June 1976.

32 Robert Goldstein, 'The Dark Side of Bette Midler', *Village Voice*, 21 April 1975, p. 127.

33 *ibid.*

34 Frank Rich, 'The Gay Decades', *Esquire*, November 1987, p. 90.

35 NBC's "Now, with Katie Couric", 18 August 1993. Midler's position at the center of the mainstream is underlined by the use of her music in the current film *One True Thing*. Her recordings of songs she introduced at the Continental Baths are the favourite music of the thoroughly conventional housewife played by Meryl Streep.

36 Bette Midler, *A View From a Broad* (New York: Fireside, 1980), p. 39.

37 Midler paid further tribute to her first audience by calling her 1998 album *Bathhouse Betty*, and filling it with the kind of eclectic program of songs she would have performed for the men at the Continental. It is either a sign of how blasé audiences have become or how historically-removed we are from the gay bathhouse heyday that the album's title has elicited little comment.

38 Stephen Holden, 'Midler, Closer to the Mainstream But Still Creating Quite a Splash', *New York Times*, 16 September 1993, C16.

8 The Moebius Strip
Act and Imitation in English Pantomime Performance

Robert Cheesmond

Of the many paradoxes and puzzles surrounding English Pantomime, one of the most obvious is why it continues to thrive as it does. As we enter the twenty-first century there is no sign of any abatement in the popularity of the genre. Despite the proliferation of cartoon versions of the fairy tales, vastly more explicit sexual displays in a variety of performative and non-performative media, commonly and continually available video and computer games, and so on, Pantomime still subsidises the year's work in many theatres, and is responsible, along with the West End Musical, for the surprising fact that in this country more people attend live theatre performances than football matches.

The many reasons why this should be so form the basis of my present programme of research, and, taken altogether, are too large a subject for this chapter. For present purposes I would like to propose that, on closer inspection, there should be little surprise at the present buoyancy of Pantomime. Far from being outdated, it accords perfectly, in several respects, with the general cultural condition which we presently experience, which we have termed (still for a while) 'Postmodernism'. This term, of course, has been variously and exhaustively defined by many scholars, whose words do not demand reiteration here. Most appropriate in the present case is Baz Kershaw's recent reminder, invoking both John Frow (1997) and Gerald Graff (1997) that:

> some of the cultural changes that 'post-modernism' signifies are certainly real, but the idea that it marks a new phase in the history of the world should currently be treated with vigorous caution, as it may best be thought of as a seductive fiction.[1]

I would suggest that Pantomime has been quintessentially 'postmodern' throughout its history, or at least since John Rich danced as Harlequin through mock-up butchers' and milliners' shops in eighteenth century London.

At a recent conference convened by the Scenography Group of the International Federation for Theatre Research,[2] a recurrent theme was that one manifestation of post-modernism in theatre has been the steady confluence since the mid-twentieth century of theatre as 'imitation of an action' and performance as action itself – variously called 'Performance Art', 'Live Art', 'Actuals', 'Happenings', and so on.

Approaches to theatre deriving ultimately from Aristotle – particularly semiotic analyses – depend upon the separation of reality and 'fiction'. So, to give one example, from Eli Rozik:

> The description of fictional reality is the ultimate objective of acting, the spectator is basically requested to shift his inferential activity from the performing reality to the fictional one.[3]

One of the essential features of Pantomime is that this distinction is by no means clear-cut; act and imitated act become the 'two sides but one side' of a moebius strip, along which the spectator – more nearly Boal's 'spect-actor' than in any other genre, except Forum Theatre itself – travels in a spirit of joyous make-believe. I suggest that this is not the 'willing suspension of disbelief', but a combined state of belief and non-belief, paralleled in our times by the *virtual reality* (an oxymoron perfectly appropriate to Pantomime) of the computer game. In what follows I focus on some ways in which this finds expression in Pantomime performance.[4]

Virtual Reality

I have a privately made video, given to me by Berwick Kaler[5], of the 1996/7 pantomime at York Theatre Royal, a version of *Mother Goose*. At a point near the end, after the power to lay golden eggs has been magically removed, Priscilla (the goose, for non-initiates) is now laying ordinary goose eggs. One is taken by the villain, Lergy, played by David Leonard, and thrown, with an unnecessarily high trajectory, to be caught by the Dame, Gertie, Mother Goose, played by Kaler.

The surrounding characters gasp.
So does the audience.

Kaler, making a great show of catching the egg, focuses upon it, and, of course, the audience. In an exaggerated cooing tone, and with much appropriate grimacing, he delivers the following:

Kaler:
> Did the nasty villain throw you VERY high up in the air, expecting me to drop you? But I didn't, did I? Nooo, I wouldn't do that to you....
> It'd make you go all scrampy scrawly....yes, all flippy woppsy...

He looks indignantly at the villain, who interjects

Leonard:
> 'Struth, she really *is* past it.

A few moments later, just before his final demise, Leonard barks at Kaler:

Leonard:

>   Get on with it, you ad-libbing old has-been!

I will return to the incident of the egg later. However, the references to Mother Goose/Kaler being "past it" have formed a leitmotif through the pantomime, along with various jokes and references to how many of the York pantomimes the various cast-members have appeared in, and whether they'll get a job next year. These are all staples of Pantomime, at least in those theatres where the show is locally-produced. The joke has less force (and relevance) to the big 'bought-in' productions such as those on the E & B circuit. In York, the audience takes enormous pleasure in its collective familiarity with the performers, many of whom have returned for successive years.

At an earlier point in the same pantomime, an exchange between Kaler and Leonard takes place on a less ambiguous level of reality. The transcription below includes indications in bold type where the actual dialogue on the video is indistinct. This does not, I think, make any material difference in the present context.

Kaler has appeared with a carrier bag over his head, because Mother Goose has been made aware of her 'ugliness'. At the point at which she is persuaded to make the deal which will give her access to the magic pool (i.e. sale of the goose to the villain, Lergy), she appeals to the audience:

Kaler: *(to audience)*

>   You don't want me to sell me goose for beauty treatment, do you, babbies?[6]

Audience:

>   No.

Kaler:

>   They don't want me to part with me goose.

Leonard:

>   Very well, then Gertie , just sign this contract saying you won't sign this contract, and out of the goodness of my heart, I'll still let you bathe in the pool.

Kaler:

>   Ooooh...too kind!

Leonard: *(take to audience)*

>   Well I could do with a good laugh! *(laughs)*
>   (*second take*) Couldn't we all! *(laughs)*

Kaler:

>   Here...(*infected by laugh. both corpse*) [7]
>   What do I do to get to the pool...**le ghoul**!

96

Leonard:

>Well, you just, er *(coughs)* 'scuse me. You just…

Kaler:

>Temperature rising, is it? *(mimes feeling forehead)*
>Ooooh! *(mimes fanning his own face)*

Leonard:

>You just…

Kaler, shooing him back, says something indecipherable. Leonard, losing concentration, takes a pace or two back to regain control.

Leonard:

>You just, er, place the, er,…

Kaler:

>Yes?…Carrier bag!

Leonard:

>Carrier bag…yes…you place that carrier bag over your head...

Kaler: (*throughout, grunting, nodding, mugging to audience*)

>Mmmmm?

Leonard corpses again.
Kaler makes nasal noises, makes an indistinct remark.
Leonard takes a breath to speak.

Kaler:

>Message coming through

Leonard starts to speak…

Kaler:

>Can't wait for the next *(indistinct)*

Leonard:

>You, er…

Kaler:

>Yes, *(sounds like)* **Rodney**

Leonard at this point admits to having lost the thread, turns to the wings, back again:

Leonard:

I can't remember…

Kaler:

erm, yes…pool!

Leonard:

That's… pool

Kaler:

Yes! Pool! Pool!

Leonard:

You, erm, place the pool…no…carrier bag..

Kaler:

Carrier bag! Pool!

Leonard:

You place that carrier bag over your head, Gertie, and you count to ten…

Kaler:

(sounds like) **You should have phoned this one in**

Leonard:

And before you know it...

Kaler:

Yes!

Leonard:

You'll be bathing in that…

Kaler:

(sounds like) **No, not really…** .

Leonard:

You'll come out of that pool, Gertie...

Kaler:

(sounds like) **Yes, Rodney**

Leonard:

You, Gertie…

Kaler:

(*sounds like*) **Yes, Rodney**

Leonard:

… will be young and beautiful!

Kaler:

Yes!

Throughout the exchange, both actors corpse, but the pattern is clear. Kaler repeatedly subverts the attempts of Leonard to deliver the lines. His technique here and very frequently elsewhere is to let the other regain some control and, at the point of the intake of breath prior to speaking, to interject. Commonly, his interjections have a rhythm of their own, a crescendo pattern with a climactic punchline. In the course of every pantomime I have seen at York, Kaler has put most of the other characters through the same (apparent) ordeal.

I have made the point that the nucleus of performers at the centre, particularly Kaler, Leonard, Martin Barrass, and Suzy Cooper, have worked together in successive pantomimes, and there is therefore an expectation that passages like this will occur. Frequently one or more of them will 'challenge' Kaler, or one another, in a similar way; cast members appearing for the first time at York are mercilessly tormented, particularly by Kaler, in a ritual which the audience, many of whom are regulars, and a high proportion of whom are adults, eagerly anticipate, knowing full well what is to come.[8]

Nevertheless, as in the case of the egg, part of the enjoyment for the audience is the sense that this is unrehearsed – as, in each individual case, it may well be – and that they are witnessing a genuine contest without a predetermined outcome, and the genuine discomfiture of one or more performers. Whatever the extent of that, the act of 'corpsing', by definition, takes place in the performing moment; the (poorly) suppressed laughter is genuine, and acknowledges the person behind the character.

So hugely do audiences at Pantomimes enjoy this experience that the 'offending' actor is frequently rewarded by a round of applause – as, commonly, are accidents with props or malfunctions of scenery, which are eagerly awaited, not in the disdainful spirit in which English students watch out for the quivering scenery in Australian soap-opera, but in a genuine spirit of willingness to celebrate the unexpected and intractable. What in 'straight' theatre would be an annoyance, a serious defect in performance, is in Pantomime inverted, expected and enjoyed.

I have argued elsewhere[9] that this subversion of the solemnity with which the-theatre-as-art is invested (at least in this country) gives 'ordinary' people, for whom at other times live theatre has no appeal, a permission to enjoy, and a sense of belonging, in an otherwise alien situation. Like television shows such as *The Big Breakfast*, similarly based on ad-libbed humour and a challenge to the 'rules' (indeed, the very concept) of 'quality television', the Pantomime is an exercise in reflexive ridicule perfectly in keeping with the postmodern cultural condition. Those who identify this characteristic as a deficiency, either of the genre as a whole or of any particular performance, as does, to offer only one example, Allen Sadler's 1992 review of *Dick Whittington* at Plymouth:

> Can British pantomime only survive by pulling its own leg? In *Dick Whittington* at the Theatre Royal, Michele Dotrice is a dotty fairy in funny spectacles and Patrick Mower rasps and rants as King Rat. The whole show is undermined by the subversive running commentary from Les Dawson as Ada the Cook, pointing out the ridiculousness of the role, the story and panto tradition.[10]

are, I suggest, simply missing the point.

Audience Ownership/Audience Control

Naturally, as we are dealing with Pantomime, the truth behind the game is more complex. Granted, the game of corpsing, by definition, takes place in the moment of performance, and reminds the audience of their situation, and their collective identity. They are empowered and given 'ownership' of the performance event. This extends, however, only to a point, and provides a site for further apparent contradictions. Berwick Kaler has on one or two occasions asked individuals to leave the theatre when

Mother Goose at York Theatre Royal (1996). Photograph: Simon Warner

'participation' took the form of offensive interjections – on one occasion by a child. Nor is the apparent glimpse of the actor behind the role entirely straightforward: the striding, ranting, raucous Geordie is a persona adopted by Kaler as a vehicle for the performance as Dame; Kaler's other self, as York audiences might be surprised to discover, is genteel and quietly-spoken, and certainly unlikely to attempt to subvert a fellow actor's performance.

An example from another theatre illustrates perfectly the delicacy of the system of relative tensions between audience 'ownership' and audience control. At Nottingham Theatre Royal, Kenneth Allan Taylor is in much the same position as Berwick Kaler at York. He has played the Dame, and written and directed the annual pantomime, for many years. The 1996/7 pantomime, coincidentally, was also *Mother Goose*.

On the night I attended, in the course of a schoolroom scene, the cast wandered off the script. The gags in the scene included mock spanking, administered by Mother Goose to adult male performers dressed as children. Apparently spontaneously, one of them shifted blame for the small transgressions to Colin, the Principal Boy, played by Jo-Ann Knowles in a leg-revealing 'traditional' costume. There followed a lengthy digression, in which Taylor went through the motions of ordering her to bend over. Clearly embarrassed, and to the huge delight of the audience and the rest of the cast, all of whom were laughing openly, she refused to do so facing upstage (for obvious reasons) but eventually did so as demurely as possible facing downstage. Taylor then mimed preparation for the spanking, but, before beginning, turned to the audience and offered the cane to 'one of the dads'. After much comic banter, a (red-faced) man did eventually come on stage, and mimed administering the caning. His discomfiture, and that of the actress, were manifest, and all present (including, I have to admit, myself) were convulsed with laughter. Eventually, after about a quarter of an hour of this 'business' the cast reminded themselves of where they were supposed to be in the script, and carried on.

I had held a conversation prior to this performance with Jo-Ann Knowles, in the course of which she described to me a performance which had been given to a house block-booked by a local firm as a Christmas party for its employees. That audience, therefore, had a considerably-developed sense of its collective identity prior to its arrival at the theatre. According to Ms Knowles's account, after a short time there began a chorus of catcalling, with offensive demands and obscene suggestions to the female members of the cast, and mainly, of course, to herself. This caused considerable distress to the company, who felt that on this occasion the essential 'spirit' of the pantomime had been subverted. The incident of the caning, on the other hand, highly sexually-charged as it was, had not *explicitly* surrendered its innocence. It might have done, and the fact that it did not demonstrates that the audience were aware of the unspecified (and certainly unwritten) 'rules' of the game, in which it was, therefore, an active player rather than a collective spectator. The laughter was that of an experience shared, as the actions took place in the 'real' as opposed to the 'performed' present.

So, too, did the throwing of the egg. In fact, however, this was not altogether as it seemed. Any reader thus far will wonder at the apparent coincidence through which such an accident of performance was captured on video. An audience present at only one performance has, at most, word-of-mouth information on what, precisely, to expect. The original egg was in fact a prop, which, Kaler informed me, he replaced one night with a real egg. Responding to the joke, Leonard did indeed 'spontaneously' throw the egg too high; the gag was then repeated in subsequent performances. On the last night of the run (traditionally a riot, for which one cannot simply buy a ticket; applicants' names are drawn from a hat), Kaler dropped it.

I was not there, but I have no doubt that the cast – and the audience – gasped.

Notes

1   Baz Kershaw, *The Radical in Performance: Between Brecht and Baudrillard* (London: Routledge, 1999), p. 21.

2   Conference 'Theatrical Space in PostModern Times; Concepts and Methodologies', held in Prague, June 1999, jointly convened by The Theatre Institute, Prague, and the Scenography Working Group of the International Federation for Theatre Research.

3   Eli Rozik, *The Language of the Theatre* (University of Glasgow: Theatre Studies Publications, 1992), p. 44 and *passim*.

4   An orthographical note: I have capitalized 'Pantomime' where the reference is to the genre, but not where particular pantomimes are the subject.

5   York Theatre Royal has prided itself on its 'traditional' pantomime for many years. Berwick Kaler has appeared in the last twenty pantomimes, in almost all of them as the Dame. He has also latterly been responsible for directing, and for writing the 'book'.

6   I have elsewhere discussed Kaler's repeated reference to the audience as his "babbies". See my 'Oh No It Isn't: toward a functionalist (re)definition of Pantomime' in Ros Merkin (ed), *Popular Theatres?* (Liverpool: John Moores University Press, 1996).

7   For the benefit of the general reader, it should perhaps be explained that 'corpsing' is the term used by actors to describe losing control, and laughing, when something goes wrong in the course of performance. It is both a transitive and an intransitive verb; 'to corpse' a fellow actor is to attempt to make him/her lose concentration, and laugh. It is a game most actors have played at one time or another. In 'serious' drama it is frowned upon, as it reminds the audience of the artificiality of performance and, in effect, brings the event onto a different level of reality. It 'breaks the spell'. As I argue, in Pantomime, where it is a staple source of humour, it becomes of importance in any discussion of this aspect of postmodernity in performance.

8   I must say here that this statement is not based upon statistics, but upon my own observations in regular attendances at York pantomimes.

9   Cheesmond in Merkin (ed), *op. cit.*

10   *The Guardian*, 2 December 1992, G2T, p. 4.

9 Reception of the Image

Ellie Parker

Hermeneutics and the Intentional Fallacy

Hermeneutics originally confined its definition to "the art or science of interpretation, *especially of Scripture*",[1] but the last two centuries have seen a shift in the meaning of the term so that it now embraces text in a more general sense. The hermeneuticist Gadamer, in his *Truth and Method* (1975) argues that no non-literal text has a finite meaning. It is dependent on the historical and cultural situation of the interpreter. The questions he addresses are entirely relevant to those facing a spectator interpreting theatre design:

> What is the meaning of a [scenographic] text? How relevant to this meaning is the [designer's] intention? Can we hope to understand works which are culturally and historically alien to us? Is 'objective' understanding possible, or is all understanding relative to our own historical situation?[2]

Godamer argues that all interpretation of past texts emerge from a dialogue between past and present; but this is not a simple process. The contemporary reader's cultural baggage can, literally, be *impedimenta* to understanding, as can ignorance. A young child is unlikely to appreciate the iconographic significance of a large statue of Lenin dominating the performing area. The dialogue between past and present can merge in a manner that could be considered as either confusing or enriching. For example, when drama students were asked what they thought the numbers stamped on the upper arms of the performers might suggest, one said *Baywatch*[3] and another, Auschwitz. Without being aware of the context, such a bizarre contradiction in interpretation coming from two spectators of comparable age and geo-cultural backgrounds might lead us to the conclusion that any meaning extracted from a theatrical visual image is so unstable as to be meaningless. But, once we know that: (a) this was a devised piece called *Office Jungle* about cruel animal behaviour in bureaucratic organisations; and, (b) that it was an idea coming from an actor which both the director and the designer liked, so it was adopted; and, (c) the actor's reasoning behind the idea was that, 'the office workers have had any individuality and sensitivity drained from them and are lost in a hierarchical numbers' game' – then intention within the collaborative structure and diversity of readings 'make sense'.

The 'Intentional Fallacy' is a phrase from an essay by W.K.Wimsatt.[4] In the canon of literary theory he was one of the first to propose that it is not necessarily the author who holds the key to the meaning of the text. The most famous example is that of Jane Austen describing her *Mansfield Park* as 'a novel about ordination' – a description most readers are unlikely to recognize. What Wimsatt was arguing for was critical concentration on actual performance: what the text says regardless of the creator's supposed intention. To post-Derridean literary theorists, the concept of there being no stable meaning is a given, but Wimsatt had prepared the way. His theory developed into reader-response theory where it is stressed that the reading process is a dialogue between author/text and reader; the dialogue results in the formation of a set of new, possibly different, meanings. Because theatre production is collaborative, the process of interpreting theatre is even more layered than that of constructing meaning from a novel. It is no longer an intimate dialogue between text and reader. The 'conversation' is a public debate between at least four elements – the written text, the performance text, the scenography and the spectator. The individual spectator is thus creating a meta-production influenced by what cultural experience or expectation s/he brings to this event.

Within any one audience, these cultural influences are not necessarily disparate and contradictory. As we have gathered from RSC marketing analyses,[5] there is a recognizable profile of the RSC Stratford-upon-Avon audience just as there is a 'target' audience of lesbians and gay men at the Drill Hall Theatre, London. Because the individual spectator is part of a collective – the audience – this view of the process of reader-response comes near to what Stanley Fish describes as 'the interpretative community'.

> Interpretative communities are made up of those who share interpretative strategies not for reading (in the conventional sense) but for writing texts, for constituting their properties and assigning their intentions. In other words, these strategies exist prior to the act of reading and therefore determine the shape of what is read rather than, as is usually assumed, the other way round.[6]

In a sample of responses to the RSC tour of *Henry V*,[7] via questionnaire and discussion, BTEC National Diploma Performing Arts students from Hereford interpreted the scenography within a notably agricultural/rural frame of reference (to one, "barn doors" were suggested; another sensed "autumn with the brown floor covering it looked like a forest with light seeping through the branches [sic]"; whereas an audience of school children attending the performance in their home town of Belfast not surprisingly construed meaning through a different set of experiences ["There was dead fowliage [sic] on the ground which was covered in dirt and rubbish like the war had been going on for years"]).[8]

Although I would argue for a rigorous relegation of scenography to a part of the whole kaleidoscopic process of production, this does not imply that we cannot isolate scenography as a study much in the way we may look closely at the written playtext in isolation from what we know to be the *whole* experience of theatre. Ian MacNeil has emphasized that there are no literary theories that can fully embrace scenography because it is "a bastard art form".[9] Certainly scenography is interpretative of a text, whether literary, musical, choreographic or purely performative, but it is no more a *secondary* text than Shakespeare's *Troilus and Cressida* is 'secondary' to either Homer,

Ovid, Lydgate, Caxton or Chaucer; nor is Brecht/Weill's *The Threepenny Opera* 'secondary' to Gay's *Beggar's Opera* simply because it is inspired by it or came after it chronologically. As Albery put it, in relation to the source text, design "tells *a* story but not necessarily *the* story".[10] Just as a play text exists to be performed, so a set design exists to be performed upon, in, and around, but that does not exclude it from separate and serious examination.

My objective is to examine the way in which scenography communicates meaning. Given that we are not discussing abstract art, we are confining ourselves to a written source text and that the expression is (ideally) a result of dialogue between director and designer, we can justifiably bring in the designer's own intentions. And because the work under discussion is contemporary, we are not having to battle with historical shifts of meaning. As Panofsky states in his *Meaning in the Visual Arts*: "Where the sphere of practical objects ends, and that of 'art' begins, depends then, on the 'intention' of the creators".[11]

As the audience survey indicates,[12] there was a wide variation of response to the RSC production of *Troilus and Cressida*. During the course of an interview Gunter was asked whether it concerned him that 'his' images were not interpreted in the way he intended them to be. It was explained that a questionnaire had been based on the design for this particular production, that one question asked was 'What does the set remind you of or make you think about?', and that these were some of the answers received:

(1) Bloody battle scenes; (2) Hospital waiting room; (3) Ancient city – wartorn; (4) Dali painting; (5) Dead trees; (6) Depressing and run down (sic); (7) Adventure playground; (8) The Troubles in Ireland; (9) Pornography, graffiti; (10) Boring and heavy (sic); (11) Polish Gothic Church; (12) Sarajevo; (13) Municipal rubbish dump.

Gunter replied:

It's all of that really. A lot of what I intended is alluded to there. It was certainly meant to be war-torn. It could have been any battle arena from Ancient Greece to Bosnia. The images ranged from shields to tin hats. It was an attempt to suggest what happens after seven years of war.

Is Gunter's answer satisfactory? The list may add up to form a composite ('It's all of that really'), but, to isolate a single response from the context of a list, is it possible to say that spectator number seven who created a meta-text of an 'adventure playground' might be 'wrong' – in the sense of seeing something that was not there? ("Is that a large bird? No, I'm wrong, it's an aeroplane."[13]) But the question of whether a response is 'wrong' in the sense of incorrect is an inappropriate one, for we are dealing neither with scientific data nor tangible realities so, when we ask what a spectator 'sees', we are asking what does s/he *understand by*, what does s/he *see into*. After all, it is conceivable that s/he may have been influenced by the Jane Howells' production of the Henry VI plays, for example, which were set in just such an arena; Bayldon's adventure playground exploited the visual pun of the 'theatre' as an arena or playground of war where the 'play' is 'played',[14] Or, when we note that the following question, "Did you like it/think it worked?" elicited the reply, "Yes, because they behaved like spoilt children", we appreciate the symbiosis of the production elements and how, within an interpretation of the performance text, the rendition of the actors colours the scenographic reading. If the performers act as rampaging children, the spectator will 'see' playground.

The response of number nine ("pornography, graffiti") is interesting because it implies a side-stepping from a reading specifically of the set towards a reading of the costumes – in particular, the first entrance of the suggestively leather-clad Trojans who then strip off. This spectator has made an imaginative leap from the depiction of war-damaged walls to 'graffiti' with the implication that the graffiti is pornographic. There is, *in fact*, no actual graffiti on the walls. In a sense, number nine's 'graffiti' was 'more imagined' than number seven's 'adventure playground'. Number seven has extended what was actually in front of him – a reification of the playground of war – presumably to accommodate imagined slides, tunnels, and ropes, whereas 'graffiti' was entirely fabricated. We are thus embracing the two meanings of both 'imagine' and 'fabricate', which are either to invent or to falsify.

The description "boring and heavy" might be interpreted as an unsophisticated, anti-intellectual, teenage vernacular response to the production as a whole; on the other hand, as an appreciation of what the set was trying to reflect, as Gunter points out, "that after seven years' siege yet Troy walls stand" (I,iii,12), it is entirely apposite. Both sides of the conflict were heartily bored by this stage, but the stout city walls still stood.

"The troubles in Ireland", "bloody battle scenes", "Sarajevo" and "war torn" are clear examples of interpretation meeting intended meaning to express the effects of long-lasting and irresolvable conflict.

"Polish Gothic church" suggests an example of the RSC 'returner' and presents the possibility of vicarious rather than empirical cultural influences. In 1995, the Swan Theatre was transformed into the interior of a crumbling, ancient Eastern European Church which became a war refugees' sanctuary in David Edgar's *Pentecost*.[15] The dominant image of this production was the 'war torn' back wall.

"Dead trees" poses further problems. There are no dead trees visible, although the change of scene to the orchard is indicated by the flying in of what could be construed as a thorn bush.[16] But the 'dead trees' image can be justified as a *metaphorical response*. The wording of the question was, after all, "What does the set remind you of/make you think about?" The response is an indicator of one of the main purposes of design: to set off a chain of associations in the imagination of the beholder, comparable, although not necessarily similar (the difference between metaphor and simile), to such a chain set off by its creator. Gunter illustrates the progression in the following extract. He was asked about the significance of the flown-in thorn bush, whether its function was purely practical. Perhaps the director had decided that what was needed at this point was an indicator to suggest the change of location to domestic/private *exterior* (in the text it's an orchard), or was there a meaning resonating beyond that?

106

I was influenced by the documentation of the First World War. There are no trees left alive. They are dead. The link is very strong between sex and death. The sexual behaviour of people in war is very different from that of peacetime. It's a fear of that link that has fuelled the controversy about the film *Crash*.

We have moved a long way from the Trojan war, but the links in the association chain are clear. The terms we might usefully adopt here are Derridean, particularly the notion of *différance*, (in the deferred meaning sense) 'slippage' and 'trace'. Derrida, in his challenge of the stability of the Saussurean sign (or, for the purpose of scenography, image) argues that signs differ not only from each other, but also from themselves in that their constitutive nature is one of constant displacement or *trace* – the trace left by an infinite chain of unstable re-signification within a boundless context of intertextuality.[17]

Translation of Emotional Response into Language

Apart from making a case for the separate study of image within a production, we have to acknowledge that despite audience research and informed guesses, it is difficult, verbally, to pin down the reading of image. The questionnaires were littered with crossings-out and indications of hesitancy, indecision and occasionally, debate ("I felt that it showed ... but my partner saw it as ...").[18] In published work, however, there has developed a certain glibness of description which passes as scenographic analysis and ignores any sense of *trace*. For example, this account of Hurry's set for the 1960 production of *Troilus and Cressida*:

> The set simply but shrewdly underscored the play's concerns with the shiftingness of human values and human relationships, the spiritual wasteland that made possible the physical wasteland of the final battle scenes.[19]

Ignoring the "simply but ... (effectively)" cliché still beloved by regional newspaper reviewers, it would be helpful to know *how* the "physical wasteland" was "made possible". What is meant by "wasteland" in this context? Are we in T.S. Eliot territory? It is the superficial slickness of the language here, rather than the struggling uncertainties revealed by the questionnaire, that indicate the limitations and problems of a linguistic response.

John Berger introduces his book, *Ways of Seeing*, with a powerful and lyrical case for the supremacy of the image:

> When in love, the sight of the beloved has a completeness which no words and no embrace can match: a completeness which only the act of making love can temporarily accommodate. This seeing which comes before words can never be quite covered by them.[20]

The implication is that the language of images, including scenographic vocabulary, is untranslatable into prose; that scenography has its own alternative language which, by definition, transmits in a different way, in a medium separate to the logocentric text. To an extent this has to be the case, but on the other hand, the images under discussion are selected and man-made, a result of intellect and human creativity rather than accident, which surely gives us some right to unpack them.

Choreography presents a similar problem of translation as Jenny Gilbert illustrates in her review of a Siobhan Davies dance piece:

> Like any language, (her work) has a recognisable vocabulary, phrases and grammar. Unlike any language I know, it is not designed to say anything directly at all.... The dance spoke, that was enough.[21]

Are we now anchored in the postmodern position then, that as long as *something* is communicated visually to a spectator, however difficult that is to define and whatever it is, that is 'enough'? Or is this a result of what Baugh describes as "dangerous individualism", when the scenographer has felt the need to go out on a limb, to redefine himself as either a fine artist or performance artist so that his contribution is so personal and is so highlighted that it separates itself out from the other production components, proclaiming its meaning to only a tiny minority?[22] If this occurs, might any meaningful dialogue be confined to only the cognoscenti composed of other theatre designers? Gilbert's review continues by suggesting just this élitism: "at a performance of Davies' latest piece, *Bank* (Bank of England? Bank of Violets? Banked fury?) I came under the distinct impression that the fine dancers of the Siobhan Davies company were communing with no one but themselves".

Contemporary designers and directors generally strike a balance between: (a) being concerned about clear communication of their (joint) understanding of the written text; and, (b) adopting a postmodern position – i.e. renunciating any hierarchical positioning of the creator(s) so as to allow each individual spectator (within the collective of an audience) to claim ownership of meaning.

Tim Albery's viewpoint embraces some of the questions of response encountered with the *Troilus and Cressida* questionnaire:

> If you are not trying too hard to engage the audience on an intellectual, conceptual level – the 'I see, they're telling us it's all like a concentration camp' school – and if you are trying to deal on a level of ambiguity, then you're offering up ideas which resonate rather than provide specific answers. So in that way the question of 'getting it' doesn't arise. I have found that the less academic the audience, the closer the response is to the visceral, non-intellectual one I had myself.

Dudley is worried enough by the problem of audience interpretation to go as far as to alter his work as a reaction to a misunderstanding of his intention:

> It staggers me sometimes, the assumptions people make. I did a production of *Heartbreak House* with Trevor Nunn a couple of years ago which had a backcloth representing the South Downs, overlooking the Channel – and the number of people who asked me why I

had put the play under water was astounding. I could *not* see how they saw that, but enough people read it in that way to worry Trevor [Nunn], so at the end of the preview week I repainted it.

This says as much about the hierarchical authority of the director as it does about the continuous call for unambiguous representationalism from the majority of the audience in conventional theatre contexts.

Iona McLeish is another designer concerned about 'misunderstanding', although she is careful to point out that it is not her sole responsibility if a spectator is confused:

It's not just *my* work though, is it? Once the whole thing is in front of you, the design is only one aspect. I have, for example, had a lot of criticism for my last piece, *The Women of Troy* at the National [1995]. People didn't seem to understand it. Most of the feed-back you tend to get is from theatre people as I suppose they're more likely to understand what you're on about. Sometimes it's a bit upsetting to realize that some people just aren't getting the point of what they are looking at. I did have a comment from someone about a show I did called *From the Mississippi Delta* which was something like 'what a shame that they could only afford corrugated iron'.

McLeish has also raised the question of a theatre-literate clique which Deirdre Clancy, costume designer for *Troilus and Cressida*, amplifies when she opines that the audience generally 'don't pick up the details' of subtle characterization communicated, for example, via the cut and fit of a costume:

It irritates me sometimes but the approval we all need has to come from one's peers. If it gets through to an audience, that's a bonus, but I think, generally speaking, an audience wants and expects display more than the postmodernist school of directors – and designers – realize. People ring up the RSC to ask if the production is going to be 'traditional' or in bin liners and string vests. And then they don't come if they hear the latter. They don't want to be challenged or threatened. People should tell directors this. Of course they don't.

Clancy is of course putting forward a conservative, pessimistic and generalized argument, but the issue of language and communication is contained in her point of view. But we might feel, like Edwards, that the designer should constantly be breaking new communication barriers and accustoming the spectator to challenge so that we are disappointed and concerned if, when a member of an audience sees something s/he wasn't expecting, s/he feels threatened.

McDonald has a more pragmatic explanation of why the visual constituent of so few productions is exciting and intellectually challenging. The play-safe crowd-pleasing director and/or designer is more likely to stay in work. He feels that certain directors and designers "haven't got as far in Britain as their talent suggests they should" because:

their productions don't make an audience feel comfortable. [The audience] worries that they aren't 'getting' it, that it's too clever for them, whereas there are some designers constantly in work at the moment because they make their audiences feel good. [Directors and designers] aren't challenging them.

But he too returns to the difficult question of communicating meaning ("You don't want to be totally obscure. As in any art form, it's hard to get the balance right"). If the images are worryingly incomprehensible to the majority of the audience and if the language of theatre design is communicable only to other designers, then this one aspect of production is a closed shop.

Is this unsatisfactory state of audience non-comprehension, and subsequent sense of threat, entirely the fault of the designer? What it might suggest is that the general public needs to be better visually educated generally and specifically in the language of scenography. Very few theatre critics are visually literate and, particularly compared to other aspects of production, apart from the practical handbook, there is very little published on the subject of scenography in Britain. Even performers are generally ignorant about the function and meaning of design to the point of seeing the work of a designer as an obstacle or impediment rather than as a parallel or complimentary expression of their performance.[23] Might it be possible to extend to scenography what John Berger achieved for the understanding of image in his *Ways of Seeing*?[24] Perhaps Svoboda's writing should be better translated, fully illustrated and placed on more theatre reading lists.

Open or Closed Design

Those practitioners who are concerned about how their ideas are communicating visually are not necessarily insisting on a specifically defined or confined mono-reading. They tend to celebrate scenography as an open narrative, and consider that multivalence and variation of response is an enhancement adding value to the original intention. Pountney feels that the joint responsibility of director and designer is to 'open doors'.

> A completely sealed narrative is limiting. It closes doors because it limits the audience's perception to viewing only that particular event instead of allowing the story to open out in such a way that it relates to other worlds. Music has an abstract quality which makes this possible, and so does design. The skill, for me, is to hold those two things – the narrative and the expressive – in balance. Once you are too prescriptive about how something should be interpreted by an audience you may as well be delivering a lecture. I do think some German directors are guilty of this rigidity in that they are trying to ram home some specific message too hard and so run the risk of over-defining.

Gunter makes a similar point in discussion about the problem of the 'closed' metaphor of the unit or single set. He cites as an example of 'good design' the 1996 Almeida production of Albee's *Who's Afraid of Virginia Woolf?*:

It's set in a bear pit – which is just what's needed psychologically. Because it's a very small theatre it's a very confrontational experience for the audience. That, for me, was a perfect example of director-designer collaboration.

Gunter feels that although a designer is often searching for the 'perfect metaphor' such as the Brecht/Nehr boxing ring, "all-embracing metaphors can be dangerous. They can be dead ends in that they can't develop in the way that a text develops". He agreed that designs for two previous productions of *Troilus and Cressida*, the 1960 Hall/Hurry sand pit and the 1985 Davies/Koltai desecrated country house, were open-ended and "non-realistic enough to avoid being limiting":

> The art is trying to get that balance between suggesting and dictating. Often it's the 'brilliant' designs that do this least successfully. The shows that I have been involved with that make the best theatre – those that have been fully integrated in terms of performance, direction and design – are not those that I felt have had the 'best' designs. By 'best' I mean the most technically brilliant or flashiest such as *Guys and Dolls*. I've just done *Skylight* [25] and what was so pleasurable about that was not that the end-product was spectacular – it wasn't; the design was functional – but that the visual contribution was right for the piece. And it was so well worked by Michael Gambon.

What we have returned to is the relegation of design to a part of the whole in that it can be judged only in a dynamic context not, for example, as the plywood model might be by the external examiner of the theatre design course. Instead of asking the clichéd and imprecise question "Does it work?", we should be asking "How well do the director/actors work it?" As Albery points out:

> Theatre design can't stand on its own. That's why I find exhibitions of model boxes so tedious. A model box on its own is sterile. It's dead. It has no meaning or life until something is happening within it.

David Fielding's experiences form a narrative of disillusionment and weariness that has pushed him towards becoming a director/designer (leaving the 'pure' designer behind with a changed name, Paul Bond). The problems with *Simon Boccanegra* [26] are worth quoting fully because they highlight the difficulty of communicating visual ideas not only to the spectator but in "Bond's" case, to the director:

David Fielding:
> If I design something to suggest one thing and an audience sees it as something else, is this a problem? I think the answer has to be no. Take painting as a parallel – there is no way that I will see, looking at a Howard Hodgkin, what he was seeing when he painted it.

Ellie Parker:

> Yes, but stage design isn't abstract painting and although I know Hodgkin gives his work detailed titles, surely design is linked to the whole performance text. It may not be the same narrative, but surely it is connected to it....

D.F.:

> Let's look at choice of colour. Do you remember *Simon Boccanegra*? It was a white tilted floor, half a circle surrounded by a half circular wall. The floor was white and the walls and ceiling were bright red. Why red? It was meant to be located in the twelfth century in the port of Genoa. With that brief, what images are evoked? What can the emotional response be? My intention was for the red to conjure up an imperial quality and the former glories of Rome. Why, one might argue, wasn't it purple? And did any one in the audience realize what the red was meant to signify? Did they all think it was the inside of a giant post-box? I've no idea.

E.P.:

> Do you ever ask?

D.F.:

> No. And no one ever seems to ask me.

From Daldry and MacNeil we find a militant anti-intellectual stance. Daldry is convinced that a spectator's first reaction will always be an emotional response and it is only with post-production analysis that the *feelings* become translated into concepts.

Ellie Parker:

> Are you concerned about how an audience interprets the design of a show?

Ian MacNeil:

> No. It should be an emotional experience and if you start intellectualizing about it, you fail.

Stephen Daldry:

> You have your gut reaction, then you test it intellectually. Otherwise it's sterile.

E.P.:

> So you expect a spectator simply to say, 'It made me sad/surprised', rather than 'having the house on stilts heightened its vulnerability and significantly distorted the perspective ...' – or whatever?

S.D.:

> You're falling into the trap of confusing post-production analysis with the actual experience of watching the play. And the process of *making* the play is different again.

E.P.:

> But you'd surely admit that in the *process* of putting a show together you're trying to communicate certain ideas – or feelings, if you like – however child-like. You've said that you are going on a particular journey, so what if that audience isn't going on the same journey as you? What if those ideas aren't coming across to an audience at all or that they are, but in a completely distorted form?

S.D.:

> So what? As individuals, they all bring a separate set of experiences to their understanding of the piece, so you can't legislate about their reaction. That's not to say that I'm not interested in people's views. Some people have an amazing take on what they've seen.

I.M.:

> I've got three essays by American academics in my drawer on *An Inspector Calls*, which I haven't read. I'm interested that I'm no longer interested, because when I was at university, I would have been writing stuff like that.[27]

The statement that comes nearest to admitting 'individualism' is the following from McDonald, but it could hardly be described as 'dangerous': "In the end I think the only person one can ever do it for is oneself.... You would hope that there are people out there who 'get' everything, but in the end you can only do what you believe is right for the piece at that time."

As readers, should we not celebrate the myriad of meanings that radiate so unpredictably from a scenographic text-in-performance rather than pursue the frustrating attempt to pin down response into one, or at most two, neatly folded and trimmed concepts? What Eagleton applies to deconstruction theory, its ability "to see ... reality less as oppressively determinate than as yet more shimmering webs of undecidability stretching to the horizon",[28] is surely pertinent to scenography.

Designers on Designing Shakespeare

It has became apparent that, rather than finding Shakespeare a particular challenge, contemporary designers do not feel obliged to bear the weight of Shakespeare's academic and cultural status:

> Shakespeare frightens me a bit, bores me a bit, but I think, as a designer, you should be given a free hand. You have so much choice. With so much in the text you can take any line you want. I think Shakespeare allows for an emotional response.

This attitude of Cairns is similar to Edwards':

> I go about designing a Shakespeare play just like any other. [The language] is so rich and so strong that it can take any number of interpretations. It has to be my personal, emotional response – which is not the way all directors want to work.

There are designers such as Ormerod who find the richness of verbal imagery a deterrent to attempt any visual competition. Declan and Ormerod argue that designing for Shakespeare is a process of elimination. It may be influenced by some knowledge of the original staging of Shakespeare's plays (i.e. the fact that the plays were performed with very little scenery), but the imperative is to create a contemporary aesthetic rather than adhere to any requirement for historical accuracy:

> It's a cliché to say that Shakespeare paints his own scenes and that he doesn't require scenery, but it is true that the word does it in most of the plays that we deal with. Nothing more is needed really than the actor and, say something to sit on – not even that sometimes. So you start off with an advantage that you don't really need anything. The essence of theatre is paring down to the essentials of what you actually need.... The visual side springs out of those essentials.[29]

Timothy O'Brien explored this process of stripping away in his 1968 design for *Troilus and Cressida* which had "nearly nude warriors on a bare stage",[30] with a set consisting "solely of portable pieces, such as military standards and an occasional couch. The action, therefore, took place against a black background that enhanced the sense of bleakness in the play".[31] In an interview with Kennedy in 1989, O'Brien used the term 'ritual nakedness' to describe his work at the RSC during this period, referring as much to his sets as to the costumes – or lack of them.

> The challenge for designers of Shakespeare production is to find an unfussy means of unlocking the text – of finding the right metaphor that is pliable enough to embrace more than a single idea and will speak to an audience of today.[32]

Fielding feels that there is too much Shakespeare performed too often. He is not intimidated by the poetry because:

> I find the complexity a benefit. Juxtaposition is stimulating. I enjoy putting contemporary design in Victorian theatres for example – so to make Shakespeare's text accessible I like the idea of modernizing it; I don't mean the over-specific and probably banal sort of 'let's set it in an Oxford College' idea, but it is possible to find a way which both acknowledges its time and speaks to ours. It's a question of finding the right metaphor.

McDonald feels "we should be braver":

> I've always envied the Germans their Ring Cycle, because I feel that they can say something about the state of their nation through each new production, and then I think 'Well, we have Shakespeare'.... These are the plays that can tell us about what we feel about our times now.

Undoubtedly some Shakespeare texts are capable of yielding up more specifically political readings than others. *Troilus and Cressida*, as Ralph Berry points out,[33] is a play with an interesting trajectory of directorial interpretations; from the Romantic/heroic 1948 and 1954 Stratford productions, to productions which reflect a blatantly anti-war political orientation. These extend from the time of the Vietnam war to present day.

McLeish refers to the 'freedom' of foreign cultures when she speaks of "preferring to work the other way round":

> Rather than design a Shakespeare, which has got such a weight of precedent behind it, I feel freer to explore the design possibilities of work of "the greats" in other languages. It doesn't matter if it's Sophocles or Ibsen. As long as it's a good, vibrant translation ...

Both McLeish and McDonald have made reference to a troubling fact – that some of the most interesting and challenging designs for productions over the last seventy years or so of Shakespeare have not been in England. More to the point, they have not been in the English language. One of the explanations for this is that just as the Berliner Ensemble stranglehold on Brecht productions eventually fossilized and institutionalized what Brecht had always intended to be a developing and organic process, so the "consumerization"[34] of the Shakespeare product, the relentless RSC sausage machine, tends to deaden any root and branch radicalism of interpretation. The mission of the RSC is to safeguard a standard of excellence in the speaking of the iambic pentameter according to the teaching of Cicely Berry. Bill Alexander's note to actors after a rehearsal of *Richard III* is typical of the logocentrism of the organization:

> The verse ... is seventy-five per cent of what this company is about. It is our instrument and our challenge. It would be easy if we were Russians and could have the verse roughly translated and then dazzle with images. We've got to dazzle with Shakespeare's language.[35]

As I have developed elsewhere, the design ideas based on a study of an Elizaveta Fen translation of *The Cherry Orchard* will differ from those responding to a Trevor Griffiths translation or an English language 'treatment' set in South Africa.[36] Surprisingly, in an otherwise detailed account of twentieth century Shakespeare scenography, Kennedy barely touches on the cross-cultural issue, the evident visual liberation provided by an up-dated translation of Shakespeare into a foreign tongue. He refers (briefly) to the visual conservatism of the British and their crippling, reverential attitude to 'our greatest poet'. He writes only of the flowering of new European theatres in the 1960s which created a

> visual renaissance that was unprecedented and that has not been matched in the Anglo-American tradition – at least partly because European directors and designers felt little of the responsibility to Shakespeare's text that has, naturally enough, restrained most productions in English in the century. [37]

There is a highly vocal body who is relieved that this is the case. We refer here to the majority of our British theatre critics.

Designers on Critics' Perception/Reception

Michael Billington says in the foreword to his *One Night Stands*:

> The charge I most frequently encounter today is that London critics are all cut from the same cloth: that they are predominately white, male, middle-aged, middle-class and Oxbridge educated. It's basically true....What exactly gives one the right to criticise? The short answer is: absolutely nothing.[38]

This is, in part, a response to John McGrath:

> It is next to impossible to take the existence of various different audiences into account, to codify their reactions to a piece of theatre, to evaluate a piece of theatre from within several frameworks. So what do we do? I'll tell you what most of us do – we take the point of view of a *normal* person – usually that of a well-fed, white, middle class, sensitive but sophisticated literary critic: and we universalise it as *the* response. The effect of such a practice is to enshrine certain specific values and qualities of a play above all others.[39]

Designers are united in their despair about what they see as a general visual illiteracy of theatre critics. Dudley tells of the critic's response to his design for *Schweyk in the Second World War* [40]:

> I took as a period reference the wonderful cartoons by Sir David Lowe who was the *Evening Standard* cartoonist throughout the war. Although they were photographically accurate ... they almost unanimously described them as Grosz' cartoons – it was just a lazy association game. If it's Brecht, then it must be Grosz. You can't write a letter to correct them because then you'd be accused of being pretentious and obscure, so they never learn.... Along with most theatre designers, I feel that stage design deserves an appraisal more akin to film criticism. Perhaps we should invite a whole different set of critics to see, and I mean really look at, our shows. Too often [critics] just get things wrong.[41]

Dudley is concerned with their misunderstanding of the finished product, of 'getting things wrong' factually, as is Björnson. She feels that "they're better than they were. At least you don't get the 'simple but effective' anymore":

> Generally speaking, they don't know their painters, their architects or their costume periods. Some of them are visually illiterate. I don't think critics have caught up with the fact that designers have raised their profile – their contribution is finally being recognized by the public as well as by people in the business.

Cairns is of the opinion that "their visual education and awareness isn't on a par with their knowledge of music or literature":

> Designers are often providing something fairly sophisticated – they have developed their craft over the years – whereas, generally speaking, opera critics are knowledgeable about music and drama critics concentrate on the verbal text and the performances. This isn't a problem except that they pronounce with the same authority about design and they simply haven't come on the journey with you.

MacNeil and Daldry's concern is that critics "try to separate out the experience" of written and visual text "without having earned that authority":

> They pontificate about the relationship of text to design.... They don't know about any of the thinking that has gone into creating this performance. They are only concerned with the result. They lack any visual vocabulary and they have no understanding of the craft or process involved. There's often a literary sterility and predictability in theatre criticism. I worry that their terms of reference are so narrow.[42]

Santini, who has moved between the rôles of theatre designer and art director for Merchant Ivory films, develops the theme of how narrow critics are in their terms of reference. He feels that critics do not understand the "healthy cross-fertilisation that we are getting in contemporary culture":

> How many theatre critics are watching pop video promos or even going to opera? They ought to be. Most of the audience are way ahead of the critics. The recent 'exhibition' of Tilda Swinton asleep in a glass case showed that. People who actually saw it found it fascinating, but you still got from some 'art' critics, 'Is this Art?' Does the category matter? It may be performance art or live sculpture – as long as it's stimulating, does it matter?

McLeish allows critics the "luxury" of being able, like the rest of the audience, to tune into any one level of the production (i.e. the literary/verbal) "because a production is made up of so many [levels]". But, as with the reviewer of *Women of Troy* who "wrote at length about the Greek amphitheatre":

> You can't help feeling that critics occasionally miss the point. Why over-emphasize the classicism of the piece when it seems very obvious to me that we had deliberately approached it from a contemporary political standpoint? ... I suppose you hope that critics have some understanding of what the design is trying to do.

Edwards goes as far as blaming critics for "holding back the development of theatre":

> They persist in regarding theatre primarily as literature. Secondly, an art exhibition can have a half page spread where the theatre review – even if it's the National – will have

half a column. And if you're in the regions, you have even less cover of course. It says a lot about the status of the work.

The conventional positioning of artist versus critic is an old war still being waged:

> No one asks an artist to produce work. Critics provide a valuable function at least as a sieve, at best as an interpreter, even, at worst, as a destroyer.... Best it seems, for any artist to put up and shut up. Indeed, this has become so accepted that any artist who publicly articulates the mildest disagreement with the status quo is considered insecure or a whinger.[43]

Bragg then makes a case for reversing "the repression of what could be a natural debate. We block the opportunity for intelligent intercourse". He presumably is referring to our debate. That between intention and interpretation.

Why do we expect the opinion of a theatre reviewer to be any more valid than that of any other spectator? Perhaps we do not. He (and invariably it is 'he') simply is in a position of power by virtue of guaranteed publication. Is it because he is paid, has seen more plays than the majority of the audience, or because he can write quickly? Or is it simply a marketing requirement (i.e. tickets will be sold on the basis of good or bad 'notices')? As Billington admits: "What gives one the right to criticise? The short answer is: absolutely nothing". Albery echoes this opinion:

> Critics over-rationalise. They have to, to get something down that makes sense! But I would suggest that going to the theatre or opera virtually every night of the week makes it hard to respond in an uncluttered, open fashion. There certainly isn't much evidence to suggest that critics are very knowledgeable about fine art – otherwise why would some of them have been so outraged by Antony [McDonald's] *Pelleas and Mélisande*?[44] You might hope that they would have seen it as part of an aesthetic continuum, but they clearly don't. Instead there is the usual tedious insistence about what the last version that they saw was like.

By contrast, Kenneth Tynan made higher claims for his rôle: "At any level, criticism must be *accurate reportage* of what has taken place outside you; at the highest level it is also accurate reportage of what has taken place within you."[45] Tynan seems to be claiming both an objective factual precision and a subjective emotional response – wanting to describe his cake and eat it at the same time. As designers have repeatedly pointed out, the 'judgement' of scenography by most theatre critics does not match their level of understanding of other production components – the direction, the written and the performance text.

Paul Ricoeur, the reader theorist ("the text is open to whoever knows how to read, and whose potential reader is everyone"), argues that a critic, because *he* is "tied to a certain culture and consequently, he isn't this absolute, disinterested subject, a sort of non-involved ego" has no qualification to "judge". In an interview he was asked to talk about the formulation of the triple function of the critic; to clarify, to explain and to judge. Ricoeur replied:

Phenomenology of the critic is based upon the dialectic between prejudice and prejudgement.... I believe that phenomenology only concerns, it seems to me, the first two, to clarify and to explain, because to *clarify* a work ... is to understand the internal structure of it, to see how the different codes, the different subjacent structures, hold the message of the work: then to *explain* is to put it in connection with its author, its public, its world ... which begins with discourse. I have an impression that *judging* ... would be passing judgement of what Kant has called the judgement of personal taste.[46]

Notes

1   *The Shorter Oxford Dictionary*, 1978 edition.

2   I have adapted Terry Eagleton's interpretation (*Literary Theory. An Introduction* [Blackwell, 1983], p.66). The logocentricity of his approach is highlighted by the statement in the following paragraph: "Meaning was not objective in the sense that an armchair is". To a reader of a scenographic text, there is no 'objective' armchair. Its age, style, texture, state, colour and so on will radiate a myriad of meanings.

3   Students at the Welsh College of Music and Drama, Feb 1997. This was not a facetious comment. The life-savers in this American television soap-opera have numbers stamped on their arms.

4   W.K. Wimsatt and M. Beardsley, *The Verbal Icon* (KY: Lexington A, 1954), p. 161.

5   Interview with Sian Sterling, marketing officer, RSC (Royal Shakespeare Company). Unless otherwise noted, all quotes in this chapter derive from interviews with the author. They are based on transcripts included as an appendix to *Design and Designer in Contemporary British Theatre Production*, a PhD thesis by Ellie Parker (published by University of Bristol, held in The Collection, Department of Television, Film & Theatre).

6   Stanley Fish, *Is There a Text in this Class?* (Cambridge, Mass: Harvard University Press, 1980), p.171, a reader-response theory also appropriated by Susan Bennett in *Theatre Audiences* (London: Routledge, 1990), p. 42. It is worth noting Selden's comment: "by reducing the whole process of meaning-production to the already existing conventions of the interpretative community, Fish seems to abandon all possibility of deviant interpretations or resistances to the norms which govern acts of interpretation." (*Contemporary Literary Theory* [Harvester Wheatsheaf, 1993], p. 60), and Freund: "The appeal to the imperialism of agreement can chill the spines of readers whose experience of the community is less happily benign than Fish assumes" (*The Return of the Reader: Reader-Response Criticism* [Methuen, 1987], p. 87).

7   Shakespeare's *Henry VI*. RSC tour. Leominster Leisure Centre, Oct. 1994. The Whitla Hall, Belfast, Nov. 1994. Dir: Kate Mitchell, Des: Rae Smith.

8   Study carried out by Ellie Parker with the assistance of Wendy Greenhill (Head of Education, RSC).

9   MacNeil. Theatre Design Conference, The Royal Court, 1996.

10   E.P. interview with Tim Albery.

11   E. Panofsky, *Meaning in the Visual Arts* (Penguin Books, 1970), p.36. He does continue: " 'intentions' are, *per se*, incapable of being defined with scientific precision".

12   A survey undertaken with the assistance of the RSC education and marketing departments, RST (Royal Shakespeare Theatre) 1996. Dir: Ian Judge. Set des: John Gunter. Costume des: Deirdre Clancy.

13   Reminiscent of, but opposed to the Hamlet / Polonius exchange where the similes attached to the cloud are open to interpretation - i.e. the issue is not whether either of the characters is being *factually* correct.

Hamlet:

Do you see yonder cloud that's almost in shape of a camel?

119

Polonius:

> By th' mass and tis like a camel indeed.

Hamlet:

> Methinks it is like a weasel.

Polonius:

> It is backed like a weasel.

Hamlet:

> Or like a whale?

Polonius:

> Very like a whale. (III. iii. 366)

14 The BBC *Henry VI, parts 1, 2 and 3*. 1981/2. Dir: Jane Howells. Des: Oliver Bayldon.

15 David Edgar's *Pentecost*. RSC Swan Theatre. Dir: Michael Attenborough. Des: Robert Jones.

16 Act III, ii,15. *Pandarus:* Walk here i' the orchard, I'll bring her straight.

17 Jacques Derrida, *Positions* (University of Chicago Press, 1981), p. 81.

18 Study undertaken with the assistance of the RSC Education department.

19 Samuel Leiter, *Shakespeare Around the Globe: A Guide to Notable Postwar Revivals* (New York/London: Greenwood Press,1986), p.754.

20 John Berger, *Ways of Seeing* (BBC and Penguin Books, 1972), p. 8.

21 *Independent On Sunday*, 25 May 1997.

22 Christopher Baugh, keynote speaker at Theatre Design Conference, RNT (Royal National Theatre), 23 May 1997. Note also Albery's 'definition of good design': "It's totally itself but it couldn't exist other than in this production. In other words, whatever its historical antecedence or aesthetic debt, which inevitably it has, that debt doesn't parade itself."

23 A view put forward by Ralph Koltai in his keynote speech, Theatre Design Conference, RNT, May 1997.

24 Berger, *op. cit.*

25 by David Hare. Dir: Richard Eyre. RNT 1995, Broadway 1996, Vaudeville Theatre, West End, London 1997.

26 by Verdi. ENO (English National Opera) 1987. Dir: David Alden. Des: 'Paul Bond'.

27 Ellie Parker, 'The Director/Designer Relationship' in *Plays and Players*, July 1996. Feature interview with Stephen Daldry and Ian MacNeil.

28 Eagleton, *op. cit.*, p. 146.

29 Delgado and Heritage (eds) *In Contact With The Gods? Directors Talk Theatre* (Manchester University Press, 1996), p. 86.

30 RSC at RST, 1968. Dir: John Barton. Quoted in D. Kennedy, *Looking at Shakespeare* (Cambridge University Press, 1995), p. 240.

31 *ibid.*

32 *ibid.*

33 Ralph Berry, *On Directing Shakespeare: Interviews With Contemporary Directors* (London: MacMillan, 1989), p. 43.

34 Baugh's phrase. Theatre Design Conference, RNT 1997.

35 Antony Sher, *Year of The King* (London: Methuen, 1985), p. 203.

36 Birmingham Rep., 1997. Dir: Janet Suzman.

37 Kennedy, *op. cit.*, p. 188.

38 Michael Billington, *One Night Stands: A Critical View of Modern British Theatre* (Nick Hern, 1993), p. x.

39 John McGrath, *A Good Night Out: Behind the Clichés of Contemporary Theatre* (Methuen,1981), p. 3.

40 by Brecht. RNT. Dir: Richard Eyre.

41 quoted in Ellie Parker, 'The Changing Role of the Designer in Contemporary British Theatre. Ellie Parker interviews William Dudley', *Studies in Theatre Production* No. 13, June 1996.

42 quoted in Ellie Parker, *Plays and Players*, July 1996.

43 Melvyn Bragg, *The Times*, 9 June 1997.

44 by Debussy. Opera North, 1995. Dir: Richard Jones. Des: Antony McDonald.

45 Kenneth Tynan. *Tynan Right and Left* (1967).

46 'Phenomenology and Theory of Literature: An Interview with Paul Ricoeur' in *Modern Language Notes*, 96: 5, December 1981, pp. 1084-90.

10 Theatre of Witness

Passage into a New Millennium

Karen Malpede

Always two theatres co-exist. One is spectacular, made for entertainment, and seems to be doing fine. The other, our necessary theatre – rough, dangerous, holy, immediate - requires re-imagining because as we enter the new millennium the weight of the violence of the twentieth century threatens completely to overwhelm our own abilities to cope. I'm proposing the idea of a *theatre of witness* which exists both as a not yet fully elucidated tradition of post-Holocaust playwriting and as a new aesthetic practice. These are plays that mature from the conjunction of the personal with the extremities of modern history and which make use of post-Freudian insights and strategies gained from testimony psychotherapies and trauma work with survivors of atrocity.

"For decades American literary criticism has sought to oppose 'man' and 'society', the individual against the communal, alterity against universality," Carolyn Forché writes in the introduction to her poetry anthology, *Against Forgetting: the Poetry of Witness.*[1] Forché suggests we contradict this enforced separation of what's called 'politics' and what's called 'art' by reclaiming an awareness of *the social*. The space where the individual exists within the communal, where the political impacts upon the human is, after all, the social world in which we live.

Traditionally, American theatre has been the home of (dysfunctional) family drama while European theatre has claimed history, idea, and high style. Agreeing with Forché, I'm suggesting a third theatrical form which is other than just an amalgam of American psychological realism and European intellectual drama. This is a new ritual and poetic theatre whose substance is the inner life as lived in the presence of history – a form, moreover, which by becoming cognizant of the extremity of twentieth-century violence poses the question: what does it take to be human in such an age as this?

About Playwriting

During the Gulf War, I had an experience which changed the way I thought about writing plays. I was taking a shower in my health club after a swim when I smelled a terrible odour rising up in the steam off my own skin. It was the smell of burning flesh, a smell rancid with decay and death. I got out of the shower, turned on the walkman I had borrowed from my child because I had become addicted to news of a war which I also actively opposed, and I learned that a bunker in a Baghdad suburb where women, children, and civilian men were hiding had been bombed by our 'smart' bombs.

I went home and, while the radio played the official justifications for the bombing of four hundred civilians, I wrote the 'Baghdad Bunker' monologue which later became part of the collective theatre piece, *Collateral Damage*. This was first performed at LaMama ETC in June 1991, and subsequently became the centrepiece of my play *Going to Iraq*, broadcast on radio in 1991 and staged in New York in 1992. What had happened to me in the shower that led to the writing of the monologue and, then, the play?

Perhaps it is always this way, at least with drama: something inside touches something outside, the sparks ignite, then one can begin to write. What was new in the shower was that the something inside came from so far away, from half way across the globe, in fact, up through my body *at the moment that it happened*: the Bunker was bombed, I smelled the burning flesh.

The lack of empathy for the war's victims was particularly appalling during the Gulf War. All of a sudden, a normally fairly compassionate and tolerant American people hardened and turned cold. We live in a world full of weapons of incalculable destructive forces, and somehow this fact is made even worse by the thought that use of relatively few of them can cause such quick destruction of empathy in a people who suddenly find themselves citizens of a nation which has gone to war. If the theatre has a function at the end of twentieth-century common life, surely it might be simply this: to recognize how fragile our capacities for empathy are in the face of overwhelming force, and to exercise those capacities for empathy for the 'other' and for the self so to increase our empathic strength.

In Italy, in the summer of 1991, the Dionysia World Symposium on Contemporary Drama was in progress when the first shots were fired in the war in the former Yugoslavia. I remember speaking from the podium to an audience of European and American theatre workers about my fears of a new war which had started so soon after the Gulf War's end; but no one wanted to discuss it then. We were in Tuscany, not far across the Adriatic from the former Yugoslavia, but we might as well have been on different planets. We were on the planet 'peace' while over there they had just landed on the planet 'war'.

Tremors in the Earth

Back visiting friends in Italy, Greece, and the south of France, in the summer of 1993, on an idyllic holiday with my husband, daughter, and her best friend, the genocidal 'ethnic cleansing' programme of the nationalist Serbs against the Bosnian Muslims was at its height.[2] All the while I seemed to feel the reality of 'ethnic cleansing' as if its shock waves had travelled across the Adriatic Sea, through the earth, and kept rupturing our Mediterranean paradise. The distinction I am making is between being aware that historical events are happening (reading the European edition of the *Herald Tribune* and employing primary Italian to muddle through the daily press) and feeling the impress of those same events at odd moments when one is not consciously thinking about them, like a hand reaching up through the earth to grab the inside of the guts.

At an ancient castle, where we often stay in Umbria as guests of a patroness of the arts, Ursula Corning, I walked the dirt road to the cypress grove and plotted out a play, *The Beekeeper's Daughter*, which was meant to capture the disconcerting juxtaposition I felt between an earthly paradise and earthly hell. When I returned home to Brooklyn, I was promptly stung by a bee while trying to rescue our curious puppy from the alarmed residents of a beehive that had mysteriously appeared under an old log in our backyard while we were away. The same day, I began the play.

In eight weeks of a sort of possessed and feverish writing, it was mainly done. I had never had this experience before for such a long and sustained period of time. It was kin to the writing of the 'Baghdad Bunker' monologue, because I felt that in both instances tremors in the earth had somehow linked me to events that happened in countries I had never visited among people I had never known. I was terrified of what I was doing, but all the same I felt impelled to show up each morning at the computer and let the substance of my terror issue through me. I was also enormously exhilarated, as one always is when words and characters seem to be using one to speak themselves. I was busy making conscious choices yet at the same time something 'other' was moving through me to which I had no choice but to attend.

In Italy, walking up and down the path from the castle to the cypress grove, I had been thinking about *Hippolytus* and *Phaedra* and wondering what is most forbidden today, in the realm of erotic longings within families, and what would happen if that forbidden thing could be both acted out and then forgiven. I wanted to write a play inspired by these wonderings but all the time, the feelings of the genocidal war in the former Yugoslavia kept rising through the earth and entering my flesh.

Finally, it was the union of this personal story of sexual transgression – between a poet-father; his bisexual male lover, a literary critic; and his daughter, still traumatized by her poet-mother's suicide – which joined itself to the story of the pregnant victim of genocidal rape who this same daughter, a human rights worker, brings out from the war. The island paradise where the poet lives, enjoying a late-life blooming of increased creativity and passion for a lovely young man, is abruptly ruptured by the arrival of his daughter and her pregnant charge.

Thus the heaven of late twentieth-century sexual and creative liberalism is broken by the intrusion of two women who have seen the worst of late twentieth-century nationalist fanaticism. The women come to the island in search of the beekeeper, Rachel's strange, clairvoyant aunt Sybil, who might be able to help Admira bear the child, and who has, Rachel knows, a violent secret past of domestic sexual abuse and death, the sharing of which might also help Admira to heal her broken life.

I knew I could have written a play that would have attempted to get inside the war in Bosnia by depicting unrelenting images of rape, torture, and murder, but I felt that as a Jewish-Italian American woman I had another task at hand, one that was consistent with what I could do and all along have been trying to do in the theatre. I needed to locate that nexus where what is outside the self joins what is inside; I needed to implicate myself in a war which we were all doing our best to pretend wasn't happening, and had nothing, anyway, to do with us.

The Assigning of 'Otherness'

News of concentration camps, of planned rapes and forced pregnancies, of torture and mass graves is as familiar as it is alien. We are stunned and fascinated by such messages of horror. We push them away, out of consciousness, out of contact with our bodies, until our flesh and our imaginations grow numb. We exploit, reify, and accept them by producing violent and assaultive art, a theatre of cruelty which affirms the victor/victim dyad.

Yet what has been going on in Bosnia, to citizens of a formerly tolerant and mixed civil society, presents a crisis to the possibility of democratic life and asks us to address what sort of social arrangements we want in the next century. How has it happened that people who lived together harmoniously for over forty years, enjoying much that was good in a socialist welfare state and at the same time much of the freedom of a Western European land, could suddenly, almost without warning, begin to be raped, tortured, exiled, and killed by neighbours and friends?

The Bosnian refugees I've met describe the former Yugoslavia as a 'beautiful country', 'a paradise'. When Bosnia seceded from the increasingly intolerable nationalist domination of Serbia, it did so in order to maintain a multi-ethnic, increasingly democratic state. Instead, Bosnian Muslims then became victims of a war of genocide, 'ethnic cleansing' practised ruthlessly by nationalist Serbs.

I wanted to show this war as it entered into the lives of people who seemed protected from it because, just as the Bosnians once felt an ethnic war like this couldn't happen to them, so Europeans and Americans quickly assigned to Bosnia an 'otherness'. Bosnia became a place of 'ancient ethnic hatreds', 'tribalism', 'Muslim fundamentalism', and such. I wanted to explore, through the lives of unique characters, that nexus where personal liberty is interrupted by extremity. Because this is the challenge that the terrible events in Bosnia have laid before the West.

Once more we find ourselves democratic peoples whose culture is interrupted periodically by outbursts of fascist nationalism and racism so virulent that whole populations who have been living civil lives soon become survivors, if they are able to survive at all. I wanted to look at what it entails to accept new survivors into our midst. The United States is largely a nation of such survivors and descendants; yet it is also a society increasingly polarized by its own racist legacies and increasingly threatened by fundamentalist violence from within.

Moreover, I wanted the play to give an aesthetic shape to a particular healing process because I feel that as an artist I must try to create dramatic actions which, though they arise out of the traumas of twentieth-century violence, also act to oppose atrocity with empathy. If I were to be personally psychoanalytic for a moment, I would say I have been driven by deep-seated feelings of survivor guilt. In my family, I occupied the 'privileged' position of the one who was not beaten, who was seldom verbally abused, and who was not seduced. I was the one who watched. By virtue of being born in the United States, all my life I have also watched wars occur in other countries. The attempt to interweave personal, family, and erotic stories with events that take place in the realm of current politics and history, but which can only be felt as they affect individual people, has dominated my playwriting since 1974, and has led to a theoretical fascination with what sort of theatre this is.

When the stink of dead and burning flesh issued through me in the shower at the health club and, three years later, when the reality of genocidal rape and war kept intruding on my solitary Italian walks, like a rumbling deep within the bowels of the earth which became a rumbling in my gut, I understood that the theatre of witness arises in the moment the body, itself, is entered by extremity from without.

Many writers have had no choice. History afflicted their bodies, causing them to become political exiles or prisoners, survivors or the victims of war. Carolyn Forché's anthology documents this body of twentieth-century poetry. Her own work as a poet, however, represents a parallel, complementary tradition in which the poet actively puts herself *with* extremity through her own empathic, imaginative opening of her body to receive images and sensations which though they belong to history have not yet forced themselves into her life. The poet invites awareness of extremity to intrude as sensation upon her imagination so that she might document, preserve, warn, and envisage social life.

Shoshana Felman's and Dori Laub's *Testimony: Crises of Witnessing in Literature, Psychoanalysis, and History* discusses literature, poetry, and the film *Shoah* in terms of their abilities to bear witness to the Holocaust. Felman quotes Elie Wiesel as writing: "If the Greeks invented tragedy, the Romans the epistle, and the Renaissance the sonnet, our generation invented a new literature, that of testimony".[3] She poses the question: "Why has testimony in effect become at once so central and so omnipresent in our recent cultural accounts of ourselves?"[4]

Witness through Theatre

To these documentations of poetry and literature of testimony and witness, it is possible to add description of the theatre of witness – a form of literature, moreover, which moves the bodies of live actors across a stage in front of an assembled audience.

I want to describe some essential elements of a theatre of witness using my play *The Beekeeper's Daughter* and the dissident Croatian playwright Slobodan Snajder's play *Snakeskin*. Snajder and I are certainly not the only two playwrights who have written theatre of witness,[5] but my interest here is not only in economy but in considering two plays written in direct response to a current crisis in society, the only genocide in Europe since the Holocaust. I'm writing because with this new European genocide the imagination of the West has been tested and found sorely wanting. What we might but did not learn when we said 'never again' – how to prevent or stop a virulent nationalist threat before it becomes a genocide – asks for contemplation. In what ways, then, do these two plays, written as 'ethnic cleansing' continued, address, memorialize, witness, and resist this genocide?

Snajder wrote in his review of *The Beekeeper's Daughter*, published in Croatia after the play's 1994 Italian premiere, the "brutally filled stomachs of Bosnian women now haunt the consciousness of critical intellectuals and artists like no other aspect of our catastrophe".[6] For both Snajder and myself, the nationalist Serb policy of rape and impregnation of Bosnian Muslim women for the purpose of producing 'Serbian babies' has its cultural origins affirmed in the tragic trilogy of *The Oresteia*. Athena's final pronouncement that "the parent is he who mounts" has consequences in the lives of actual contemporary women who are taken from their communities, brutalized, and outcast because they are forced to bear the child of the aggressor's rape. As

126

playwrights, we felt justified and impelled to use the theatre to address, demythologize and remythologize the story of who is the parent of the child.

Snakeskin

Snakeskin takes place in an abandoned hospital which has become a hiding place for refugees during a modern thirty years war. *Beekeeper* is set in the summer of 1993, on a Mediterranean island paradise, quite removed from and yet close to the fighting in Bosnia. In *Snakeskin*, a Muslim woman, Azra, whose name means 'virgin', is discovered dumped pregnant and half-dead in a ruined car outside the hospital by a male nurse Hasan, and carried in to Martha, "a woman who belongs to neither of the warring factions",[7] who has taken refuge in the autopsy lab in the basement.

Azra refuses to speak or eat, and wants to kill herself. Martha, and then also Hasan, confront and slowly overcome their initial resistance to Azra and involve themselves in trying to save her life and help deliver and care for her child. In a series of dreams, through which the playwright lets us into the inner life of this numbed and silent victim, the child Azra bears appears to her as a beautiful young man, a demon/tempter, asking to be born. In Martha's dream, the older woman becomes a goddess, endowing Azra with strength as she reclaims the world from 'the rule of the fathers' and proclaims a return to the mythological time of mother-right.

Just as *Beekeeper* juxtaposes the 'paradise' of the mediterranean summer against the 'hell' of the lives of victims of the war, *Snakeskin* also opposes 'heaven' and 'hell' by juxtaposing scenes of the starving refugees in their hospital with their glorious dreams. Snajder also creates scenes that take place in a literal heaven among the various gods who war with one another while their various worshippers are warring down below.

In a climactic scene, the three wise men appear on earth with an offer to purchase the child to turn him into a symbol of a new god for whom presumably new religious wars will be fought in times to come. Though for a moment Hasan is sorely tempted by the easy cash and a way out from the responsibilities of parenthood, he joins Martha in her refusal to sell the child. Azra is still too numb to enter the debate. Like Joseph, the earthly father of Christ, Hasan decides to become a caring parent of his non-biological child. In this holy trinity of sorts, is Azra the Christ figure, sacrificed to redeem our sins, or is it her child? Snajder shows how, as victim and as woman, Azra is absent from history. In a courtroom scene that recalls both the legendary trial in *The Eumenides* and looks forward to the War Crimes Tribunal, Azra sits silently, buffing her nails. In a final scene, though, Azra revives, to go with Martha and Hasan in an attempt to rescue the now grown son from 'a ruling military regime of a sort of planetary Palestine' where he is being trained to become an agent of revenge.[8] But as the young soldier tries to shed his military uniform (his 'snakeskin') and join his mother outside the barbed wire, both he and Azra are killed by shrapnel.

Snakeskin seems true to what we know of history since it supposes an inevitable cycle of revenge in which well-intentioned individuals might intervene for humanistic reasons but which they will be powerless to avert until and unless our cultural myths are changed. Is Snajder, a male playwright, actually longing for the new matriarchy?[9] He's clear, in any case, that patriarchal father-right has led us to genocidal rape.

The Beekeeper's Daughter

In *The Beekeeper's Daughter*, the educated, cosmopolitan, and secular Bosnian Muslim Admira Ismic (named after a young woman who was killed presumably by Serbian snipers while trying to flee Sarajevo with her Serbian lover) is brought by an American human rights activist, Rachel Reichenthal, to her poet father's island retreat. Like Azra, Admira wrestles with alternate suicidal and infanticidal urges. Unlike Azra, Admira finds herself a refugee in the peaceful West by virtue of travelling the few hundred miles to the island.

Very pregnant and very traumatized, Admira at first tries to appear normal when introduced to her hosts, but she soon finds herself the victim of terrifying flashbacks. Rachel, the human rights activist, also attempts to appear 'in control', but falls victim almost immediately to impulsive outbursts of rage directed at her father's bisexual lover, her father, and even at Admira. Only her aunt Sybil escapes, but that is because Rachel puts enormous pressure on Sybil to take over Admira's care. The presence on the island of Admira and Rachel brings the trauma of the war into the lives of poet-father, literary critic/lover, and beekeeping aunt in ways that affect their feelings, their bodies, and what they do with both.

Just as *Snakeskin* alternates between scenes in heaven and on earth, and between dream and waking life, so *Beekeeper* finds a dramatic structure to uncover progressive layers of the unconscious as scenes move from the domestic limits of the house, to a pastoral but sexually charged picnic near the beehives, into the primeval forest where characters finally act out the sources of their traumas, and towards the ultimate purification of the sea. The language of the play intensifies accordingly, becoming with every scene more revealing of the inner life, as if the intensity of each witnessing crisis compels each character to speak closer and closer to the core.

Like Hasan in *Snakeskin*, the poet Robert Blaze (a Robert Gravesian student of the feminine source of creativity) assumes the role of parent to the new-born child of rape. The obsessive joy with which he becomes involved in nursing the baby threatens and transforms his relationships with his lover and his daughter. Admira can't touch the baby; Rachel and her Aunt Sybil are completely involved with Admira's care, until Admira's flashbacks so terrify Rachel she runs into her father's lover's arms. In the forest, Sybil and Admira are finally able to tell and hear one another's tales.

At the end of *Beekeeper* Admira and her child are alive and she is sculpting a monument of mother and child called "the survivors". Rachel is back at work gathering testimony for the War Crimes Tribunal, and is pregnant with a child which might have been fathered by Jamie, her father's lover, or may be the result of her relationship with the Sarajevan journalist she has since married. Biological fatherhood is unclear. Rachel, like Admira, will choose the male caretaking parent.

Both these women's renewed lives are possible only because their testimonies have been received by empathic others. Hence, *Beekeeper* presents a challenge to those outside the genocide. If healing is to happen, the testimony of the victims of 'ethnic cleansing' (including that of human rights workers) must be heard and allowed to enter into and so alter the hearers' lives.

Both these plays show how the ability to bear witness challenges the 'idea' which led to the actual rapes being planned, ordered, and carried out as a systematic part of 'ethnic cleansing'. Serbian nationalists who rape Muslim women do so in order to destroy the fabric of Bosnian society by creating female outcasts who give birth to 'Serbian babies'. Women have been made to sing Serbian nationalist songs during their rapes. Women's fingers have been cut off their hands, leaving them permanently in the shape of the three-fingered Serbian nationalist salute. The rape of women has been videotaped and circulated as pornography. But in these two plays the children born of rape are felt, by the characters and by the audience, to be the children of their Muslim mothers, whose bodies bear babies and the memories of the torture of their rapes. Moreover, the prerogative of male parenthood is redefined not as 'he who mounts' but as *he who cares for the living child*.

A Bosnian Muslim refugee, herself the mother of three children she rescued from the war, said to me after watching a rehearsal for the first New York production of *The Beekeeper's Daughter*: "All Bosnian women should see this play because it proves to her that the child is hers no matter where it came from". In both *Snakeskin* and *The Beekeeper's Daughter*, the Christian, Jewish, and Orthodox characters defy the idea of 'ethnic cleansing' by sheltering and saving a Muslim woman and a child.

The Witnessing Imagination

The term 'witnessing imagination' describes a way of seeing violence which produces acknowledgement of and also resistance to the human cost of violence. The witnessing imagination thus seeks to give form to the multiple dynamics which occur between the victim of violence and the person who provides the holding empathic environment in which the story of the violence might unfold. The witnessing imagination *sees into violence* because it focuses upon *the inner life* of the individual who has been inside the violence as its subject. By so doing, the witnessing imagination tries to revive the integrity of the inner life which the violence sought to annihilate. So if violence is the attempt to turn a person into a thing, the witnessing imagination attempts to turn this 'thing' back into a person.

The psychiatrist Dori Laub writes that "the Holocaust was an event without a witness",[10] hence it could not be known as an actual occurrence even by those who survived it. Laub, himself a Holocaust survivor, records the videotaped testimonies of other survivors, preserving their words both for themselves and for history. Stevan Weine, dramaturge for *The Beekeeper's Daughter*, a psychiatrist and co-director of the project on Genocide, Witnessing, and Psychiatry, works alongside Bosnian and Croatian psychiatrists to record the testimonies of Bosnian victims of the nationalist Serb-sponsored genocide. Weine writes:

> Witnessing defines an interdisciplinary approach for working to counter trauma's destructive effects on self and society. Witnessing gives shape to the complex psychological, historical, and cultural processes of recovery from the collective traumas of genocide, war and oppression.[11]

If bearing testimony allows the individual to reclaim the self, the witnessing of such testimony also reclaims the victim's experience for the society of which the individual, by virtue of being heard, can once again become a part. The inner life of the 'despised other' which genocidal violence seeks to annihilate, once and for all, without a trace, is quite literally *reborn* through the efforts of the witnessing imagination. Even if the individual has perished, if the utterance has survived, in poem or play or testimony, testament to the inner life survives. As Carolyn Forché writes, "the poetry of witness reclaims the social from the political and in so doing defends the individual against illegitimate forms of coercion".[12]

We see how in the theatre of witness of the two plays, *Snakeskin* and *The Beekeeper's Daughter*, the historically verifiable destruction of women by the act of genocidal rape is moved against by the force of the playwrights' witnessing imaginations. Each play suggests a social alternative to the shame, alienation, exile, infanticide, or suicide of the women raped and children born of rape. But this is an alternative that is only possible if others outside the immediate violence enter in – to listen, hear, and help.

In each play, witnessing characters recognize the mothers as wounded women who need nurture (food, starvation, and self-starvation are images and themes in both). The fact of being seen, although it can often be vastly uncomfortable for the women victims, nevertheless allows the two Bosnian Muslim women and the human rights worker to begin a struggle with their own suicidal and murderous impulses. Also, in each play, witnessing characters recognize the integrity of the children, and claim them as legitimate members of their own societies. The recognition of the babies by others allows the two mothers to begin to move towards a recognition of these children as their own.

In *The Oresteia*, the cycle of revenge is finally ended by recourse to an arbitrary, convenient, wrong-headed, and – if the physical integrity of the body is paid heed – patently absurd, ultimately (in the light of genocidal rape) dangerous, legalistic decision: "The mother is no parent of that which is called/her child, but only nurse of the new-planted seed/ that grows. The parent is he who mounts. A stranger she/ preserves a stranger's seed...." But precisely because witnessing pays attention to the body – to what the body has endured and to what it knows – we can now suggest that the witnessing imagination might work far more effectively to end the cycle of revenge than ever did the tragic imagination.

In witnessing dramas, characters bear witness with motives based upon self-interest. The characters in both plays are driven by needs, desires, longings, and losses from their own pasts. Martha in *Snakeskin* is the mother of a son who was killed in the war; Azra's pregnancy offers her the chance to mother again. Rachel Reichenthal, the human rights activist in *Beekeeper*, needs to save others in order to make peace with her own mother's suicide; her aunt Sybil mothers Admira because she was once responsible for her own daughter's death, the result of a car crash in which in a moment of madness she meant to kill herself and her child as a way to escape from the domestic prison in which they were being battered and abused. Robert Blaze was a distant father to Rachel – too wrapped up in his art and difficult marriage to pay her much attention; the new baby offers him a chance to relive what he missed at a time in

130

his life when he is able to value caretaking. Admira in her agony reminds Robert and his daughter of the tortured poet wife and mother who killed herself; caring for Admira allows them both to come to terms with this past death.

Altruism and Mutuality

If these characters happen to perform altruistic deeds, they do so, also, to achieve their own well-being. Witnessing propels characters in different ways; it cannot always be assumed that what they do will directly benefit one another. Sometimes characters, while intending to help, inflict hurt. Enduring suffering and causing suffering are part of the witnessing dynamic. So is simply being overwhelmed and unable to take in or speak another word. In *Beekeeper*, Rachel's need to heal Admira makes her go too fast and put too much pressure on Admira; she rages when Admira won't tell her the whole tale. Sometimes, as in *Snakeskin*, external violence defeats all attempts at bearing witness. The moment the grown son decides to put down his arms, he and Azra are killed.

It is probably significant that these two plays were written by writers who are outside the experience of genocidal rape. Slobodan Snajder, a Yugoslav from Croatia, is a man who cannot experience forced impregnation; I am a woman but an American. Snajder, of course, has been inside the war and so he set his play inside a war zone in which all the earthly characters are also war victims. Both of us, though, set out to imagine a witnessing scenario that hasn't happened yet. Most women who have given birth to children of genocidal rape have wanted nothing to do with their babies, and there are stories of the babies being sent to Serbia to live in orphanages. The aims of the genocidal policy are being achieved when the abandoned babies are thought to be 'Serbian', and when their Bosnian Muslim or Croat mothers are forced to be silent about what they have endured in order to be reintegrated into their own cultures.

The reality can even be more grim. A Croatian mental worker told Stevan Weine she had cared for four women who were victims of rape. The four women gave birth, and disowned the children; two of the women then committed suicide, and the other two attempted suicide. But before we blame the playwrights for their unrealistic treatment of the facts, we could ask ourselves whether or not it might help if the witnessing imagination were so prevalent that the women victims of genocidal rape were able to be met (as the characters are in the plays) with an extended social family that struggles to accept both the babies and the mothers, and struggles to see neither baby nor mother as outcast, as shamed, unwanted, dirty, or anything less than totally desirable. It is, after all, the function of the theatre of witness to set the elements of the witnessing imagination before the public, so that they might be considered and, perhaps, embraced as actions within the realm of human possibility.

The Socializing Dynamics of Theatre

Don't assume, either, that the playwrights have written these plays because they are any more altruistic than anyone else. I don't know Snajder very well. I saw him over the course of a week at the Dionysia Festival. But I can hazard to say that both of us are haunted by deeply-rooted feelings of never having been adequately seen or recognized. Much of our conversation in Italy, over cappuccinos and wines in beautiful cafés, was about how badly we are treated as artists in our own countries; how we cannot get our plays produced at home.

What's underneath these feelings of being permanently outcast and pariah-like (aside from external situations in both our countries that militate against our work) is the subject for a long analysis. Suffice to say here that I think we both write witnessing drama because its subjects are completely fraught for us. I know from teaching so many young students, as well as from living my own life, that few people have escaped being personally affected by the traumatic, often random, violence of the twentieth century: so many people are refugees from war; so many others are victims of violent homes, of sexual assaults, incest, or rapes; still others have seen friends and relatives die violent, needless deaths; and there is virtually no one now who has not witnessed the slow and difficult death of someone close to them from cancer or AIDS, the archetypal diseases of our age. Even those who have managed to lead completely sheltered lives have seen televised images of genocide and war. Everyone in the world lives under the cloud of possible nuclear annihilation and/or ecocide. For virtually all of us, then, the challenges of witnessing must seem relevant, immediate, necessary.

The Greeks understood the centrality of theatre to social life when they made attendance at the City Dionysia mandatory for citizens of the fledgling democracy. Likewise, the theatre of witness might occupy an uniquely necessary place in the social life of contemporary democracies. The poet of witness distils the experience of extremity into image. The poetic act, the making of the image, is proof that the experience entered into the poet's own sentient awareness.

Reading poetry, we find ourselves one with the poet, feeling what was felt, seeing what was seen. Poetic language, the language of image through which thought and feeling are joined, is important to the theatre of witness. In theatre, though, an additional dynamic becomes possible, one in which the audience is able to witness the act of witnessing as it takes place between characters.

The theatre audience becomes implicated not only by the force of accumulating images, but also and additionally because it is receiving information about what takes place between the teller and the listener during the testimony encounter. The audience sees how witnessing affects all parties to the tale, and their position outside the dialogue allows audience members to move between empathic identification with the body of the one whose testimony is being offered and the one whose body is being entered by the testimony. The audience becomes not only witness to the testimony, but witness to the witness of the testimony.

Is this position any different from the one the spectator of a drama usually occupies? The answer is, yes, most definitely. The difference is quite simply this: if inside the play itself there is no one capable of bearing witness, no one who hears, sees, and takes into the body the truth of the other's story, the audience is let off the hook, so to speak, since it can then perceive no possibility of witnessing, and hence no real resistance to violence. Such an assault upon the senses, which is quite the stuff of much political theatre influenced by Artaud's Theatre of Cruelty, serves to reaffirm the inevitability of state-supported violence and genocide and the ultimate hopelessness of the human condition and of the individual within it.

The witnessing imagination, however, in its essential abilities – to reveal the inner life as a place of resistance to violence; to show how the suffering history inflicts on individuals can be both told and heard; and to reclaim the social world of human discourse from the political world of force – implicates the spectator in these transformative possibilities. Since witnessing challenges history, becoming party to the witnessing encounter challenges one's own view of one's own place in, and even responsibility for, history and one's own understanding of the validity of individual sentient awareness in the face of history. If witnessing suggests an alternative, it is an alternative that can only be *felt inside the bodies of those who see*. Thus the witnessing imagination breaks down alienation, despair, ennui by enlivening the flesh itself.

The Crises of Witnessing

What the body feels comes to it in the form of *crisis*. The witnessing crisis is proof that the witnessing imagination has validity, force, and transformative power. Shoshana Felman describes those in the throes of a witnessing crisis as being

> entirely at a loss, uprooted and disoriented, and profoundly shaken in [their] anchoring world views and in [their] commonly held life-perspectives ... Suddenly – without a warning – [the experience of listening to trauma can] shake up one's whole grip on one's experience and one's life.

Listeners may pass through "the crisis of experiencing their boundaries, their separateness, their functionality, and indeed their sanity, at risk".[13]

The witnessing crisis is an experience well known to mental health and human rights workers who receive the testimonies of survivors of genocide. When Stevan Weine read *The Beekeeper's Daughter*, his work receiving testimonies from Bosnian refugees fitted him immediately to perceive the play as a story of the witnessing crises in the lives of the five characters.

Witnessing crises are inherently dramatic. They are also different from the more traditional drama of *the agon*, the conflict between two opposing forces. Within the witnessing dynamic, characters might, indeed, come into bitter conflict, and yet their main trajectory is not to conquer or to triumph one over the other, nor is it finally to realize their own vulnerability as they stand distraught over the bodies of the ones they loved but killed, nor to reveal their own isolation and failure to connect to any other living thing. The witnessing crisis shatters and reorients the inner life around cognizance of an extreme reality the body was once too traumatized to be able to receive. Through witnessing, the full ramifications of atrocity are allowed to surface, but in a safe environment.

Memories of what the body and the soul suffered dawn, and with them comes an awareness of who this new self – a self that has endured, remembered, and born witness – is and might become. A witnessing drama does not coalesce around a single climactic moment. Witnessing is a process, raising questions, revealing possibilities; witnessing crises rise and fall, like waves in the sea.

If a witnessing crisis affects and stimulates the playwright, it also affects and stimulates actors in rehearsal, and ultimately, the crisis is shared during the performance with the audience. In each case, the witnessing crisis presents an ordeal through which one passes, and during which one perceives a real danger to the heretofore known and understood boundaries of self. In rehearsal of *The Beekeeper's Daughter*, at various times various actors underwent a crisis of witnessing which altered not only their understanding of their character and role but also their knowledge of their own inner life and memories.

Thus, the actress who played Sybil had a stunning understanding the day before the Italian premiere of the play which made her shake with terror when she faced the large audience on the first night – which severely damaged her opening performance, but enriched all later ones. She had abruptly understood the reason for her own mother's madness, a seemingly inexplicable reality which traumatized her childhood. Her mother had been driven mad quite like Sybil in the play, through horror at the brutality inflicted on her by the man she had loved. It was by entering the character that the actress also, simultaneously, had entered the reality of her mother's life which had been hidden from her.

The young actress who played Admira struggled to keep her own rape experience unexplored within her because she felt that nothing she had endured could in any way approximate the horror of Admira's torture. One day, Stevan Weine, our psychiatrist and dramaturge, who worked consistently with me and the actors to understand the crises proffered by the play, told this young actress that virtually every survivor he had ever interviewed kept their own memories at bay by insisting that whatever they have suffered is not worth acknowledging since it cannot have been as terrible as what others have endured. This information allowed the actress to let in the reality of the memories of her own rape, and thus freed her, giving her at once renewed compassion for herself, and a true familiarity with Admira, so that many more or less stylized movements and attitudes she had adopted to play 'the victim' could now fall away.

The Break with Tragedy

In theatre of witness, a dramatic action takes form which reconnects self to deeper, previously hidden layers of self; connects self to the other; and provides a renewed connection to the social world. This happens through a series of activities that allow for hearing, remembering, memorializing, sharing, teaching, philosophizing, confronting, comforting, revealing, grieving, and feeling a continuum between one's pre- and post-traumatic life. Thus, theatre of witness results in the formation of new community, however fragile, and fraught.

Theatre of witness paradoxically also provides the decisive break with tragedy which modern and postmodern tragi-comedy has been unable to achieve, and it resonates most closely with ancient tragedy because of the extremity of its situations, the densely layered imagery of its language, and its clarifying impact on its audience.

From my experience watching audiences watch *The Beekeeper's Daughter*, I can say that they knew that something unusually powerful had happened to them. Inevitably, a few people close off to this experience and damn the art that brought it about, but many more report an effect that does not leave them, so that, seven months after our small workshop production closed, audience members are still coming up to all of us involved to say that the play lives on inside them in ways they are unable to forget, and to ask when they will be able to see the play again.

Such a powerful, lasting, unforgettable response on the part of many in the audience is an affirmation of the power of partaking in the witnessing imagination as a necessary and desired – hence, consequential – experience for people alive at the end of the century. "For the first time I feel I am not alone in the world," Ivica Boban, the brilliant anti-war theatre director and creator from Croatia said after she had seen the play. Doug Hostetter, who runs the Bosnian Student Project, said: "How did you know? This is exactly what we've all gone through".

Audience members not directly involved in the Bosnian war more typically reported that by allowing them a way to feel-through their thoughts about Bosnia, the play had brought them into contact with aspects of their own lives which had seemed incommunicable before.

The Millennial Moment

Fitting, isn't it, that the twentieth century which has been so utterly extreme is about to exhaust itself in the dawn of a new millennium? This conjunction of its violent legacy with the promise of a new age has already stimulated a fundamentalist religious revival, a 'born again' desire to 'bear witness' to the second coming of the messiah which is sweeping through the monotheistic religions and in various ways is challenging the cosmopolitan, secular, democratic, tolerant, feminist, and eco-conscious tradition from which much modern art and modern resistance to totalitarianism have been made.[14]

But the millennial experience, far from being monopolized by an apocalyptic, doomsday, doctrinaire scenario, might actually be about secular social witnessing. Social witnessing focuses upon the seeing of people. Such sight of one's god as might appear is visible through the quality of relationships that people are able to have with one another and with the sentient world in which they live. Secular witnessing does have a spiritual component, quite naturally, but it comes without fundamentalist ideology. One is free to believe and be according to one's own light.

The imperative to bear social witness to the ways in which the self, in its personal and social aspects, manages to exist within and to resist the genocides, nuclear terrors, state-sponsored deaths, and lethal diseases of the century may be the only fitting way to bid this century goodbye. Witnessing in the theatre, as in testimony forms of psychotherapy, provides the I and Thou experience. Witnessing affirms connections based upon the human capacities to experience compassion and empathy for the self and for the other as powerful, motivating forces.

A theatre of witness increases the individual's and the society's capacity to bear witness. By putting the witnessing action and its crises before us, alive in time in space, the theatre of witness provides its audience with the knowledge, the courage, the time, and the community in which to contemplate and affirm its engagement in actual, private and public acts of witness. Those for whom witnessing might be a daily job – human rights, health, mental health, and social workers; artists, teachers, journalists, lawyers; and, also, one might add, parents, and friends – are affirmed in the validity of their tasks, and receive the energy that live theatre can transmit when it gives shape to actions that resonate inside the body.

In my own case, I knew no Bosnian refugees until after I had written *The Beekeeper's Daughter*. Like almost everyone else, I was made vastly uneasy by the thought of knowing people whose historical misfortunes were so completely overwhelming. The work on the play brought Bosnian refugees into my life not as 'unfortunate others' but as colleagues and friends who offer both self and story. To say that my own personal life, and that of my family and of the theatre company with which I work, has been enriched by my Bosnian friends is only to state what people engaged in the human realities of this war already know. The meeting with so many profoundly gentle, intelligent, friendly, quietly dignified people brings home the awful waste of war like nothing else. The human encounter with history's victims tests and renews one's own humanity. Quite simply, life seems duller and less worth the effort without such witnessing encounters and, witnessing comes therefore to seem quite simply something that presents itself for doing at this time on earth.

In many ways, the special interest identity politics of the last twenty-five years have prepared for way for witnessing. Needing to define ourselves by race, gender, ethnic origin, sexual orientation, nature of disease or disability has shown us how to recognize both self and other. Witnessing takes the step beyond the politics of groups

which otherwise ends in fragmentation and isolation; the witnessing encounter joins across the divide of discrete experience. Letting the self be changed by communion with the other's situation and tale, taking into the body the sensations of another's struggle, simply being present

The picnic scene from Karen Malpede's The Beekeeper's Daughter in the premiere production at the Florence Mission Project studio theater, New York City, 1995, during the war in Bosnia. The poet, Robert Blaze (George Bartenieff) holding the baby born of a Serbian rape, stands behind the three women (left to right): his human rights activist daughter, Rachel (Carolyn Goelzer); Admira Ismic (Christen Clifford), a Bosnian rape victim who is comforted by Sybil Blaze (Lee Nagrin), the beekeeper. Photograph: © Beatriz Schiller.

to hear and so allowing words to form and be spoken, enlarges and revitalizes each individual involved in the witnessing experience and reaffirms the social contract.

And witnessing is exciting, even dangerous. It presents a crucible in which the self is fractured and reformed. The witnessing crisis becomes the liminal space through which one passes and from which one might emerge quite changed. Social witnessing, in fact, may be the authentic galvanizing ritual experience of the passage through the end of the twentieth century.

The survivor, the one who testifies, has become the spirit guide for us. The survivor's stories tell us what has happened in the innermost recesses of the human heart, when the self has met annihilation and yet continued to give voice, to sing. Our ability to listen carries us along, makes us one with an almost mystical effort to resist coercion, dehumanization, and the silencing of the inner song. If witnessing appears to us now as organic, authentic, millennial ritual, the theatre stands to be enormously revitalized by its embrace. Furthermore, we might conclude that the millennial moment requires a theatre which will externalize and communalize this innermost need by giving witnessing dramatic action and shape.

Acknowledgement

"Theatre of Witness: Passage into a New Millennium" first appeared in *New Theatre Quarterly*, Volume XII, No. 47, August 1996. Copyright © by Karen Malpede. We thank the editors and publisher for permission to reprint it here.

Notes

1   New York: Norton, 1993, p. 46.

2   See, among other sources, Roy Gutman, *Witness to Genocide* (New York: Macmillan, 1993); and *War Crimes in Bosnia-Hercegovina*, two volumes (New York: Helsinki Watch, 1993).

3   Shoshana Felman and Dori Laub, *Testimony: Crises of Witnessing in Literature, Psychoanalysis, and History* (New York: Routledge, 1992), p. 6.

4   *ibid.*, p. 10.

5   Snajder and I met at the 1994 Dionysia World Festival of Contemporary Drama where *The Beekeeper's Daughter* premiered. The play opened as a sold-out workshop in New York the following February, and was staged in Australia in May 1996. Theater Three Collaborative in collaboration with Other Pictures produced *The Beekeeper's Daughter* at Theater Row Theater on 42nd St. in New York City, in February 1997. The production was directed by Ivica Boban, a Croatian theatre director. *Snakeskin* was to be the centrepiece of the Dionysia festival in September 1995, after its German premiere.

Among the playwrights who might be said to have written at least one play in the tradition of theatre of witness are Yeats, O'Casey, Augusta Gregory, Lorca, Stein, Lillian Atlan, Nellie Sachs, Ariel Dorfman, Caryl Churchill, Athol Fugard, Nzotake Shange, Tony Kushner, Hélène Cixous, Emily Mann, Larry Kramer – a far from exhaustive list.

6   'Sto Moze Kazaliste?' in *Novosti*, 30 July 1994, p. 29, trans. Jasna Perucic as 'What Can Summer Festivals Do?', unpublished. In this article, Snajder also wrote: "I want to assert unequivocally that this play is one of the most honest representations of our tragedy I have encountered so far.... I was deeply moved by this play, although in actuality, the play deals with 'their' problems, not 'ours'. But the world is homogeneous in its tragedy."

7   Author's notes to *Snakeskin*, unpublished manuscript, trans. Niccoleta Gaida.

8   *ibid.*

9   This, in any case, is a phrase he uses to describe his experience of watching *Beekeeper*, so the longing, at least, is on his mind.

10 Felman and Laub, *op. cit.*, p. 75 ff.

11 Stevan Weine, unpublished preface to *The Beekeeper's Daughter*, 1994, pp. 3-4.

12 Forché, *op. cit.*, p. 45.

13 Felman and Laub, *op. cit.*, pp. xvi-xvii.

14 See Charles B. Strozier, *Apocalypse: on the Psychology of Fundamentalism in America* (Boston: Beacon, 1994), for the study of this phenomenon.

Contributor Biographies

Lorenzo Buj holds a PhD from the University of Michigan, Ann Arbor. He teaches art theory and criticism at The University of Western Ontario (Canada), and publishes frequently on issues in contemporary art and cultural history.

Robert Cheesmond worked as a professional director and designer before joining the Drama Department in Hull University in 1974. There he has pursued an ongoing programme of practical research into performance and presentation, combining this with a study of popular and non-literary theatre forms, in particular English Pantomime. An active freelance practitioner in a variety of contexts (most recently as designer to a presentation of *Cinderella* in a class B prison), he is also a convenor of the Scenography Working Group of the International Federation for Theatre Research.

Henry Daniel is Artistic Director of Full Performing Bodies, a performance company based in Winchester (UK). Born in Trinidad, West Indies, he worked as a young actor with poet/playwright Derek Walcott at the Trinidad Theatre Workshop prior to extensive touring as a dancer with many professional dance companies in the USA and Germany, including the Jose Limon Dance Company of New York. He currently lectures in Performing Arts at King Alfred's College in Winchester.

David Jiang worked as a director and an actor in China for more than twenty years, and has continued both his academic and practical drama career since he acquired his doctorate degree at the University of Leeds. He is currently teaching in the Theater Department of Barnard College at Columbia University in New York.

Ruru Li was raised in a Peking Opera actress family and received some early basic theatrical training. Her research interest lies in comparative and intercultural theatre studies, and she has published works on Shakespeare in China and Chinese theatre. She is now a senior lecturer of Chinese Studies at the University of Leeds where she also teaches Theatre Studies.

Tony Lopez has published many books of poetry including *Abstract & Delicious* (1983), *A Theory of Surplus Labour* (1990), *Stress Management* (1994), *Negative Equity* (1995) and, most recently, *Data Shadow* (Reality Street, 2000) and *Devolution* (The Figures, 2000); his first American book was *False Memory* (The Figures, 1996). His poems may be found in the major anthologies *Conductors of Chaos* (Picador, 1996) and *Other: British and Irish Poetry since 1970* (Wesleyan University Press, 1999). He is Reader in Poetry at the University of Plymouth.

Karen Malpede is a playwright, screen writer, director, and human rights and trauma worker. She is author of several books, including *Women in Theater: Compassion & Hope* and an anthology of early plays, *A Monster Has Stolen the Sun and Other Plays*, as well as many articles which have appeared both in theatre and psychology anthologies, the *New York Times*, *New Theatre Quarterly* and elsewhere. She is the winner of numerous grants, including a Ludwig

Vogelstein Foundation Writer's Grant, CAPS Grant for Playwrighting, a PEN Writers Grant, and the McKnight National Playwright's Fellowship, given annually to writers whose work has had an impact on the American theatre. She co-founded New Cycle Theater and is currently a co-founder of a small production company, Theater Three Collaborative, Inc. Her most recent projects are a screenplay about Emily Dickinson, *I Emily*, currently under option in Hollywood, and a stage adaptation of Victor Klemperer's *Diaries of the Nazi Years*. She is completing her first novel.

Roberta Mock has directed, designed, and devised many experimental, absurd, or avant-garde plays since 1992. She is a founder of Lusty Juventus physical theatre for whom she co-directed *Shading the Crime* and *Ceremonial Kisses*, both by Christine Roberts, as well as directing the European premiere of *Us* by Karen Malpede. Her theatre reviews and feature articles have appeared in *Time Out*, *The Independent*, *The Guardian*, and *Scotland on Sunday* and she has contributed academic articles to *Studies in Theatre Production* and *New Theatre Quarterly*. From 1990 to 1995, she was editor of the avant-garde literary journal, *massacre*. She is Subject Leader of Theatre & Performance at the University of Plymouth.

Ellie Parker is a performance practitioner and director of her own company, New Theatre Works. Her PhD centred on contemporary British scenography and she has been published in several academic journals as well as in more popular ones such as *Plays and Players*.

Christine Roberts teaches Theatre & Performance at the University of Plymouth. A trained actor, she has also written seven plays for theatre and is a founding member of Lusty Juventus, for whom she wrote and co-directed *Ceremonial Kisses* and *Shading the Crime*. Her latest play, *The Maternal Cloister*, about Sor Juana de Inez de la Cruz, is currently being produced by Theatre Carnivalesque. She has also written for international journals and delivered conference papers on themes relating to theatre and politics.

Ruth Way trained at London School of Contemporary Dance, Merce Cunningham Studios (New York) and studied voice with Meredith Monk. She has performed internationally with Earthfall Dance, devising and choreographing three of their major works. She is a founder of Lusty Juventus and has choreographed and performed in all of three of the company's productions. Ruth has taught contemporary dance and physical theatre skills extensively throughout Great Britain and is a lecturer in Theatre & Performance at the University of Plymouth. She is a co-director and head of choreography at Cygnet Training Theatre.

Kevin Winkler is Chief Librarian of the Circulating Collections of the New York Public Library for the Performing Arts, where for a number of years he was Assistant Curator of its Theatre Collection. He is currently Vice-President of the Theatre Library Association (TLA). A former professional dancer, he holds a B.A. in theatre from San Diego State University, an M.A. in theatre from Hunter College, and an M.S. in library science from Columbia University. His articles have appeared in *Theatre History Studies* and *Performing Arts Resources*.